Margaret Picton

Understanding Design in the Home

Illustrated by Doreen Lang

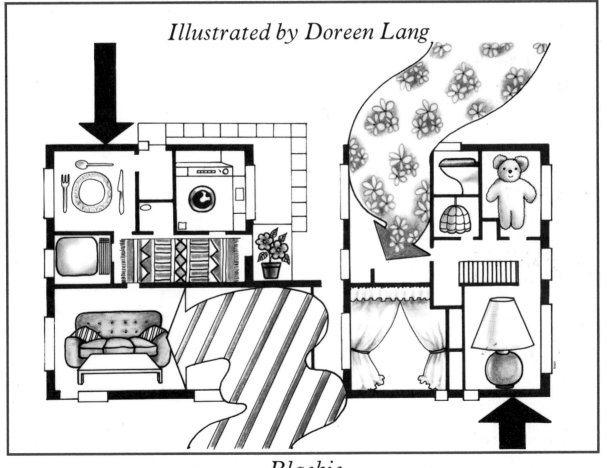

Blackie

BLACKIE & SON LTD
Bishopbriggs · Glasgow G64 2NZ

●

Furnival House · 14–18 High Holborn · London WC1V 6BX

Printed in Great Britain by
Cambus Litho, East Kilbride

Contents

Acknowledgments

The author and publisher would like to thank the following for permission to reproduce copyright material:

British Standards Institution for the kitemark and safety symbol on page 1

British Electrotechnical Approvals Board for their symbol on page 1

Paraffin Heating Advisory Council for their own symbol and the symbol of the Oil Appliance Manufacturers' Association on page 1

Timber Research and Development Association for the "Touch Wood" symbol on page 89

National Association of Retail Furnishers Ltd for their symbol on page 89

What is "good design"?

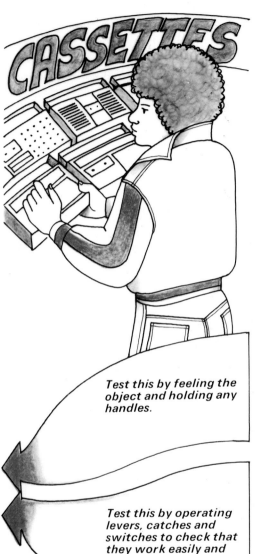

Each time you go shopping you have to make some important decisions. Shops stock a variety of goods and you have to look around and choose the article you think is best. You may be tempted to buy something which is eye-catching and very fashionable, or a product you have seen advertised on television. This may not always be the best buy and you may find that you have spent your money on an unsuitable or badly-made article which quickly becomes a poor bargain.

A study of design helps you to recognize quality. It makes you aware of the good and bad features of any product and helps you to select wisely when you go shopping.

The design of an item can be analysed (examined) by considering three factors:

1 Use or function
2 Quality, durability or value for money
3 Appearance

Use or function

Look at the item and ask yourself the following questions.

a What is it intended to do?
b Is it likely to do its job well?
c Will it be easy to use and comfortable to handle?
d Are the operating instructions simple to understand?
e Are control knobs and switches correctly placed for ease of movement and for safety?
f Has the item been approved by a Consumer Protection body? Look for the labels which show that it has passed approved safety tests. Here are some:

Test this by feeling the object and holding any handles.

Test this by operating levers, catches and switches to check that they work easily and efficiently.

BS 5258

g Will the item be easy to clean and simple to maintain? If spare parts are required will they be readily available?

h Is the item suitable for the age and ability of the consumer (user)?

If your examination of the item suggests that it will do its job well, then it can be described as ***functional***.

Quality, durability *or value for money*

Look at the item carefully and ask yourself the following questions.

a Does it look well made?

b Has the item been made from a material suitable for its purpose?

c Is it likely to last? To decide this you must consider the age of the consumer and the type of treatment it will receive.

d Does the price seem reasonable, bearing in mind the materials that have been used? To get an idea of a fair selling price, compare the price of the item with that of several other similar products, preferably from different shops.

If your examination of the item suggests that it will last well, then it can be described as ***durable***. If, in addition, the price seems reasonable then the item should be good value for money.

Appearance

Look at the item and ask yourself the following questions.

a Does it look attractive? Does the shape, line, colour, pattern and texture appeal to the sight and touch?

b Has the item any features which you think are unnecessary or could be improved upon?

c Do you like the item enough to want to buy it for yourself?

d If you buy the product, do you think you will still like it in a few years' time?

If, after considering all these factors, you decide that the item is functional, durable and pleasing in appearance, then it can be described as an example of ***good design***.

Check that there are no weak parts that can be damaged easily or broken.

Try not to be influenced by the latest fashionable trends. Remember that a durable product should last for a long time.

The work of the Design Council

The Design Council is a government-sponsored body which receives an annual grant from the Department of Industry. Its work consists of:

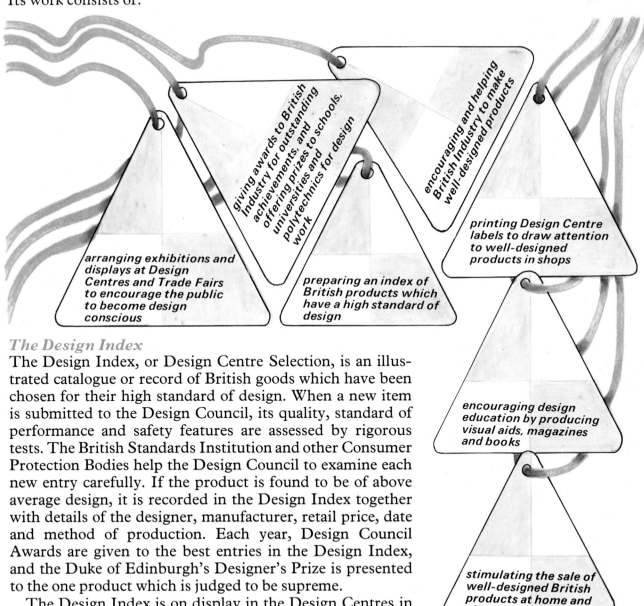

arranging exhibitions and displays at Design Centres and Trade Fairs to encourage the public to become design conscious

giving awards to British Industry for outstanding achievements, and offering prizes to schools, universities and polytechnics for design work

preparing an index of British products which have a high standard of design

encouraging and helping British Industry to make well-designed products

printing Design Centre labels to draw attention to well-designed products in shops

encouraging design education by producing visual aids, magazines and books

stimulating the sale of well-designed British products at home and abroad

The Design Index

The Design Index, or Design Centre Selection, is an illustrated catalogue or record of British goods which have been chosen for their high standard of design. When a new item is submitted to the Design Council, its quality, standard of performance and safety features are assessed by rigorous tests. The British Standards Institution and other Consumer Protection Bodies help the Design Council to examine each new entry carefully. If the product is found to be of above average design, it is recorded in the Design Index together with details of the designer, manufacturer, retail price, date and method of production. Each year, Design Council Awards are given to the best entries in the Design Index, and the Duke of Edinburgh's Designer's Prize is presented to the one product which is judged to be supreme.

The Design Index is on display in the Design Centres in London and Glasgow, and also at the Liverpool Building and Design Centre. It can be viewed by anybody wanting information on well-designed British goods.

Design Centres

The two main Design Centres are in London and Glasgow, but there is a smaller showroom in Cardiff. The Design Centres arrange displays and exhibitions of selected products from the Design Index. There are room settings showing examples of well-designed furniture, fabrics, tableware, household appliances, wall and floor coverings etc., and also exhibitions on particular subjects or themes.

The Centres are open to the general public and admission is free. Each Design Centre has a bookshop selling Design Council books, magazines and pamphlets, and a shop selling a small range of well-designed products, with the emphasis on good-quality British souvenirs.

Design publications

"Design", "Engineering" and "Craft" are three magazines published by the Design Council and there is a series of Design Centre books on various aspects of planning and furnishing a home. The monthly magazine of the Consumers' Association, "Which?", gives valuable information on points to look for when choosing furniture, fittings, household appliances and manufactured products. Why not visit your school and local libraries to look at copies of these publications?

Careers in Design

If you are interested in finding out about careers in Design, visit your school and local libraries, or ask your careers teacher for advice.

Here are some useful addresses:

1 Design Council, 28 Haymarket, London SW1Y 4SU
2 Design Council Scottish Committee, 72 St Vincent Street, Glasgow G2 5TN
3 Design Council Wales, Pearl Assurance House, Greyfriars Road, Cardiff CF1 3JN
4 Liverpool Building and Design Centre Ltd, Hope Street, Liverpool 1

5 Consumers' Association, 14 Buckingham Street, London WC2

6 Crafts Council, 12 Waterloo Place, Lower Regent Street, London SW1Y 4AU

There are many interesting careers available in the field of Design. Usually designers are trained at a college of art and design, or at a college of technology, engineering or architecture. Here are some of the skills in which designers can specialize.

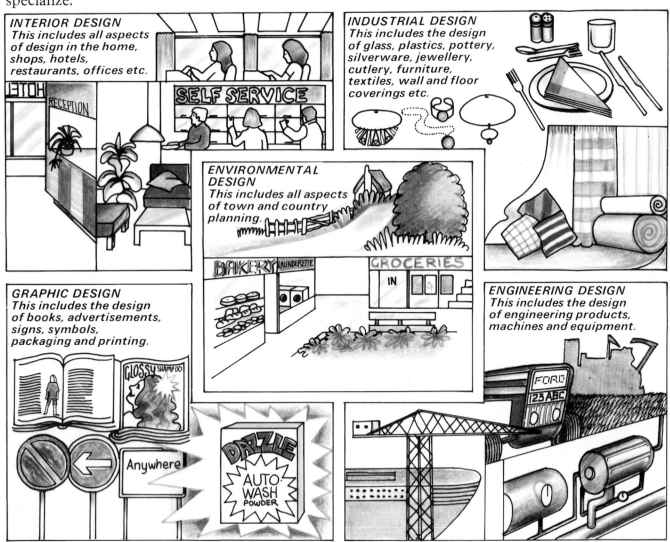

INTERIOR DESIGN
This includes all aspects of design in the home, shops, hotels, restaurants, offices etc.

INDUSTRIAL DESIGN
This includes the design of glass, plastics, pottery, silverware, jewellery, cutlery, furniture, textiles, wall and floor coverings etc.

ENVIRONMENTAL DESIGN
This includes all aspects of town and country planning.

GRAPHIC DESIGN
This includes the design of books, advertisements, signs, symbols, packaging and printing.

ENGINEERING DESIGN
This includes the design of engineering products, machines and equipment.

Housing

From earliest times people have built houses to:

give shelter from the weather

provide defence against wild animals or warlike enemies

Pictures of early men hunting animals have been found scratched on the walls of caves in Europe. In some of these cave drawings there are primitive huts or houses—the earliest recorded forms of man-made shelter.

In the past, men looked for house sites near wells or springs, so that they would have a good source of water. They looked at the soil to see if it was porous and had good drainage, and to see whether it was fertile enough to grow food in. Nature told them if the area was healthy. If animal and plant life thrived, then it was likely that humans would too. In Britain nowadays, clean water is piped to most areas and a main drainage system disposes of sewage, so houses can be built almost anywhere.

House designs vary from place to place and from country to country. Climate influences housing. Where there is a lot of snow or rain, houses are built with steeply sloping roofs and very wide eaves. In very cold countries thick walls are needed for insulation. Try to find out other ways in which climate has influenced the design of houses.

Materials which are available locally are often used for building houses. Mud brick, bamboo and long grasses are still used in many areas in Africa. Timber is used in forested regions such as Scandinavia, Canada, Switzerland and Austria. Try to find out about the local building materials available in your area.

Housing design is also influenced by the building techniques known at the time, and the needs and likes of the people. Early houses tended to be plain, functional and often uncomfortable. Gradually it became fashionable to have decorative and ornate buildings. Today's trend is back towards simplicity in design, use of colour and decoration.

The Tudor or early modern age was characterized by an interest and pride in house building. Brick, wood and local stone were used to build magnificent houses. Large fireplaces with brick chimneys were fashionable, and windows had small panes of glass set in lead strips. Ordinary homes, too, had glass windows, and large ingle-nook fireplaces with seats on either side of the fire. Steep spiral staircases led to the rooms upstairs.

During the seventeenth century Christopher Wren and Inigo Jones were two architects who influenced the look of houses. Their designs were simple, elegant and beautifully proportioned. The Great Fire of London in 1666 gave them a marvellous opportunity to redesign London along classical lines. Houses were built with magnificently carved staircases, panelled walls and high painted ceilings. Grinling Gibbons was a great wood carver of this period. He was responsible for the beautiful carved woodwork in many houses and churches, including the new St Paul's Cathedral.

An ingle-nook fireplace

The Royal Crescent, Bath, in 1919

In the late seventeenth century it was fashionable to join houses together in a continuous line or terrace. The end and centre houses were often slightly different to distinguish them from the rest. This idea was developed in the eighteenth century when classical terraced houses were neatly grouped around tree-lined squares, crescents and circuses. Smaller houses were built behind, following the same design. An architect supervised the development of the town to ensure uniformity.

The Adams brothers were famous architects who designed and built beautiful town houses for the wealthy middle classes. They were particularly remembered for their doorways, elegant windows and distinctive fireplaces.

In the nineteenth century, terraces continued to be fashionable. John Nash designed and built beautiful Regency terraces in London. Houses of this period had distinctive curved or bow windows, decorated pillars and ornate trellis-work verandahs. During the late nineteenth century there was a return to individual design and large rambling houses were built in their own grounds. The Victorians delighted in fussy ornamentation and their houses were a strange mixture of pinnacles, towers and gables.

With the Industrial Revolution and the growth of the cotton, woollen, iron, pottery and mining industries, there was a demand for more housing for the poor. Rows of "back-to-back" company houses were built for the workers. These terraced houses were cramped and dark, and usually consisted of two rooms downstairs and two rooms upstairs. There were no bathrooms and the front door of each house opened into the living room. There were communal yards with a cold water tap and a dry earth closet or cesspool nearby. The primitive sewage system and the damp, overcrowded and unhealthy living conditions resulted in frequent outbreaks of diseases, like scarlet fever and diphtheria.

In 1875 a Public Health Act was passed which made it compulsory for the plans of all new buildings to be approved by local authorities. Houses had to have damp-proof walls of a certain thickness, and a proper drainage system. There had to be a lavatory outside the back door, and a copper boiler

Back-to-back workers' houses with an open cesspool running between them

which heated water for washing clothes or filling the zinc bath. These town houses were sturdily built but badly planned. They still had small, dark rooms and long, dark corridors.

In 1890 the Housing of the Working Classes Act allowed local authorities to build houses, and London and Liverpool were amongst the first to undertake large-scale council building schemes.

When railways were built it became possible for people to travel to work, and so houses were built on the outskirts of the overcrowded towns and cities. Well-to-do people preferred to live in these new housing districts or "suburbs", and detached and semi-detached houses and bungalows were built with front and back gardens.

During the early part of the twentieth century, private and council housing estates were built in large numbers. Houses were often positioned along main roads and would stretch into the open country. This was called "ribbon development". Government regulations were eventually introduced to protect the countryside by preventing ribbon development in "green-belt" areas. Most new houses of this period had a bathroom, an inside lavatory and a hot water supply. Electricity had replaced gas for lighting, and either gas or electricity was used for heating and cooking.

AEROFILMS LTD

An example of ribbon development

In towns and cities, where building space was limited, towering blocks of flats were built. These high-rise flats were made possible because of new building materials and techniques. High-rise tower blocks provided homes for many people but they were found to be inconvenient, cramped and lonely places, especially for old people and families with young children. Medium-rise flats of up to eight storeys have become more popular.

Houses today are simple in shape, and light and airy. They are often built in groups in landscaped surroundings.

Modern building materials and methods

House builders today can use an assortment of traditional and modern materials. Brick, local stone, granite, sandstone, limestone, chalkstone, slate and wood are still used, together with new materials such as reinforced concrete, plate glass, lightweight metals, plastic, machine-made bricks and artificial stone.

Pre-cast concrete was developed in the nineteenth century, but it was only during the twentieth century that it became widely used by builders. Concrete (a mixture of gravel, sand, cement powder and water) is a cheap, strong material which is fire resistant. It can be made into prefabricated blocks in factories which are then transported to building sites and fitted to a framework of steel girders. Another method uses ready-mixed concrete which is poured into a wooden-framed skeleton of the building with vertical steel rods inside it. When the ready-mixed concrete has dried, the skeleton frame is removed.

Plate glass can now be made into large sheets and this has meant that windows are bigger, making rooms lighter and more spacious. Lightweight aluminium is often used for windows and door frames. This is a metal which does not require painting and needs little or no maintenance.

Plastics are used widely in modern buildings. They can be used for gutters, drainpipes, floors, internal plumbing fittings, work surfaces, wall coverings and furniture. Plastics do not need painting and are easily cleaned.

New building materials, together with advanced machinery and an improved transport system, have made new building methods possible. Many buildings today are prefabricated. This means that whole units are made in a factory and then taken to the site for erection. This method is sometimes called "industrialized" or "system" building. Prefabrication has many advantages.

Foundations

Ground floor

Completed 'shells'

Door and Windows

Second storey

Buildings can be made to unusual and advanced designs which would have been impossible with traditional materials.

Most of the work is done in factories so it cannot be delayed by bad weather.

Actual work on the building site is reduced to a minimum.

There is a reduction in labour costs because fewer men are needed to construct the building.

Buildings can be erected quickly.

A word about energy conservation and home insulation

Coal, oil, gas and electricity used to be reasonably priced fuels, but now they are costly means of producing heat and energy. The oil-producing countries of the Middle East have cut back on their export commitments and this has made oil scarce as well as expensive. It is therefore important to conserve (save) energy whenever possible, until cheaper alternative sources of power are found.

Home insulation helps to conserve energy by eliminating or cutting down the heat loss from a house. This means that less fuel is needed to keep the building warm. Heating rooms and providing hot water accounts for more than 80% of the energy used in homes, so home insulation can make a real contribution towards cutting down on the cost of fuel. Heat is lost from a building through the:

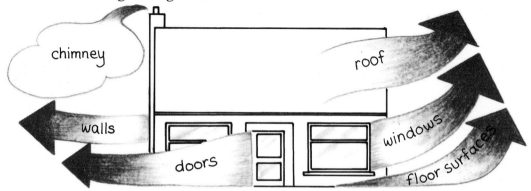

Here are some sensible and economical ways to prevent heat loss in the home.

1 Insulate the loft and trap door with a 75 mm (3″) thickness of special glass fibre insulating material.

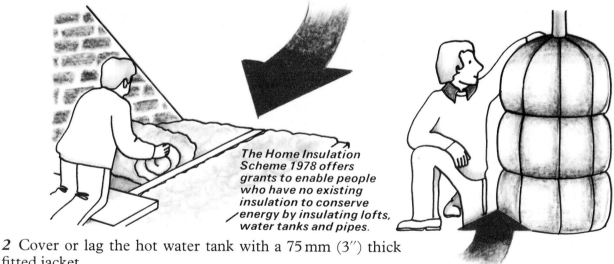

The Home Insulation Scheme 1978 offers grants to enable people who have no existing insulation to conserve energy by insulating lofts, water tanks and pipes.

2 Cover or lag the hot water tank with a 75 mm (3″) thick fitted jacket.

3 Edge windows and doors with insulating strips to eliminate draughts. Special draught excluders can be fitted to the bottom edges of internal and external doors.

4 Lay thick, fitted carpets to prevent heat loss through the floorboards.

5 Hang long, heavy curtains at the windows to eliminate draughts from badly-fitting window frames.

6 Block up unused fireplaces.

7 Keep internal doors closed whenever possible. Special hinges can be attached to doors to make them self-closing.

8 Fit a hinged draught excluder over the inside of the letter box.

Here are two expensive ways of cutting down on the heat loss from a home. It should be remembered that although the initial expense of installing these methods is high, heat wastage is reduced resulting in less costly fuel bills.

1 Install double glazing to make windows and outside doors completely draughtproof.

2 Fill cavity walls with insulating material to eliminate loss of heat through the wall surfaces. This method must be done by specialists.

Energy can be saved by using less.

1 Turn down the thermostat one degree on central heating systems.

2 Make sure that thermostats and time switches are fitted to central heating systems to make them more efficient, by switching off automatically whenever they are not required.

3 Switch off radiators in rooms which are not used.

4 Hang strips of metal foil behind radiators and cookers to reflect heat into the rooms.

5 See that all heating appliances are checked and cleaned regularly, and that flues and chimneys are swept. An efficient heating system uses less fuel.

6 Switch off lights which are not needed.

7 Bake in bulk whenever the oven is being used and store the extra food in the deep freeze, if one is available.

8 Boil only the amount of water needed when brewing tea.

9 Use the hob of the cooker instead of the oven.

10 Eat more raw vegetables and fruit instead of cooking them.

11 Use slightly less hot water in the bath or have a shower instead.

Try to be energy conscious and think of more ways of using less energy in the home.

Solar heating uses energy from the sun. The sun's energy is collected on special glass or clear plastic panels, and then absorbed by black metal plates. This stored heat can be used to heat a domestic hot water system or to provide space heating. Solar heating saves energy but it does require special equipment which can be expensive to buy and install.

A look at room plans

An architect is a person who designs buildings. He prepares very detailed drawings of his designs so that the builder knows the exact size of the rooms and how they fit together. Very few drawings are made "full size". They are usually drawn to scale, so that a much smaller version of the building is shown.

An architect prepares many different drawings of the building from different angles and positions, all accurately drawn to scale. Here is a plan showing the outlines of the walls of a house seen looking straight down. It illustrates how the rooms fit together and the positions of the windows, doors and fireplace.

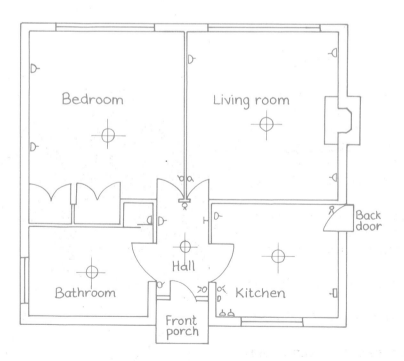

Room plans must also indicate measurements and the position of power points, light fittings and switches. Curved lines are used to show the space required for the opening and closing of doors. Here are some international architects' symbols which are used in room plans.

Electric power point

Electric cooker power outlet

One-way light switch

Two-way light switch

Pendant light fitting

Immersion heater switch

Telephone point

Look again at the room plan on page 14 and see if you can find each of these.

Very few people are able to have a home built to their own design, but many people move house sometime during their lives. This may involve scanning the "Houses for Sale" notices in newspapers, or looking at property advertised in an estate agent's office. Here are some points to look out for and discuss when viewing the plans of a property or being shown round a house.

1 Is the property connected to the main services, e.g. water, gas, electricity, sewage disposal, telephone etc?

2 Is it convenient for work and is there a reliable bus or train service?

3 Is it near enough to schools, health centres, parks, libraries and social centres?

4 Is the property big enough for the size of your family and do you really *like* it?

5 Can you afford the mortgage repayments or rent, rates and other expenses, and still be able to live comfortably?

6 Is the property in good condition? You may need expert advice on this matter but look for obvious signs of dampness, rotten woodwork or neglect.

7 Has the property a good aspect and view? Suggest some places where you would not like to live if you had the choice.

Look at each room in turn and check the following features.

Is there an electric cooker outlet or a gas pipe for a gas cooker?

Check that the floor surface is non-slip when wet.

Are the electric light fittings correctly placed? One central light does not always give adequate illumination to important areas, such as cooker, work surfaces and sink unit.

Is there adequate natural lighting and ventilation?

Are there enough power points? Check your requirements from this list: refrigerator, freezer, food-mixer, dishwasher, washing machine, tumble drier, clock, iron, kettle, heater, toaster, microwave oven, slow cooker—but remember that it is unlikely that more than three of these items will be in use at the same time.

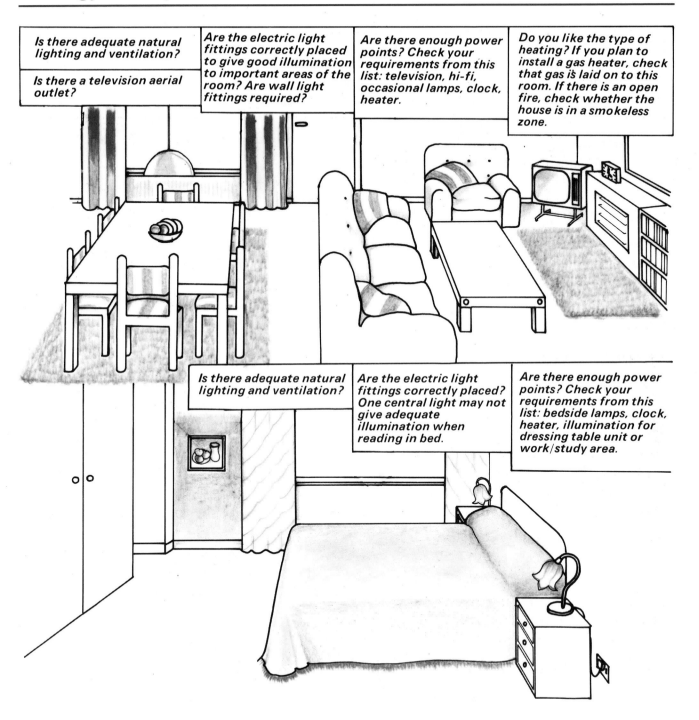

Is there adequate natural lighting and ventilation?

Is there a television aerial outlet?

Are the electric light fittings correctly placed to give good illumination to important areas of the room? Are wall light fittings required?

Are there enough power points? Check your requirements from this list: television, hi-fi, occasional lamps, clock, heater.

Do you like the type of heating? If you plan to install a gas heater, check that gas is laid on to this room. If there is an open fire, check whether the house is in a smokeless zone.

Is there adequate natural lighting and ventilation?

Are the electric light fittings correctly placed? One central light may not give adequate illumination when reading in bed.

Are there enough power points? Check your requirements from this list: bedside lamps, clock, heater, illumination for dressing table unit or work/study area.

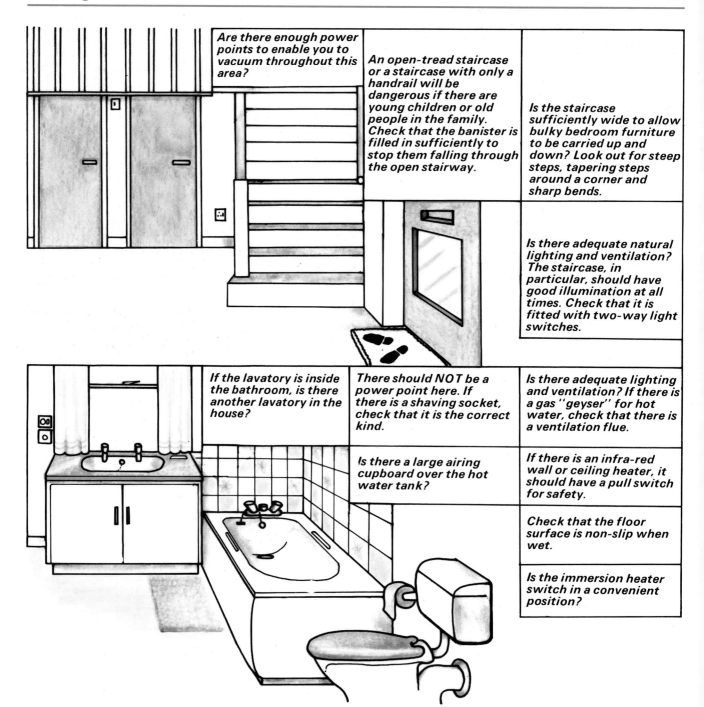

Are there enough power points to enable you to vacuum throughout this area?

An open-tread staircase or a staircase with only a handrail will be dangerous if there are young children or old people in the family. Check that the banister is filled in sufficiently to stop them falling through the open stairway.

Is the staircase sufficiently wide to allow bulky bedroom furniture to be carried up and down? Look out for steep steps, tapering steps around a corner and sharp bends.

Is there adequate natural lighting and ventilation? The staircase, in particular, should have good illumination at all times. Check that it is fitted with two-way light switches.

If the lavatory is inside the bathroom, is there another lavatory in the house?

There should NOT be a power point here. If there is a shaving socket, check that it is the correct kind.

Is there adequate lighting and ventilation? If there is a gas "geyser" for hot water, check that there is a ventilation flue.

Is there a large airing cupboard over the hot water tank?

If there is an infra-red wall or ceiling heater, it should have a pull switch for safety.

Check that the floor surface is non-slip when wet.

Is the immersion heater switch in a convenient position?

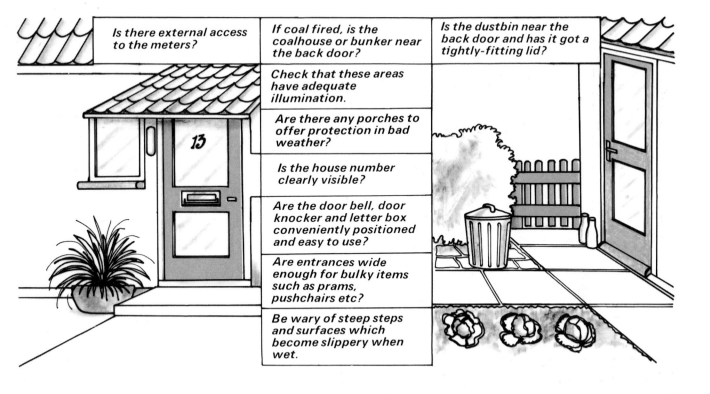

Is there external access to the meters?

If coal fired, is the coalhouse or bunker near the back door?

Is the dustbin near the back door and has it got a tightly-fitting lid?

Check that these areas have adequate illumination.

Are there any porches to offer protection in bad weather?

Is the house number clearly visible?

Are the door bell, door knocker and letter box conveniently positioned and easy to use?

Are entrances wide enough for bulky items such as prams, pushchairs etc?

Be wary of steep steps and surfaces which become slippery when wet.

Think and Do

1. Ask your grandparents or any old people in your neighbourhood if they will tell you:

a. what wash day used to be like when they were young;

b. what bath night was like;

c. some of the disadvantages of using dry earth closets.

2. Look through the "Houses for Sale" advertisements in your local newspapers. Make a list of all the abbreviations you notice, e.g. W.C., sfch, o.n.o. Find out what each one means.

3. Design a poster which will encourage people to conserve energy.

4. Visit your school and local libraries and find out all you can about *one* of the following:

a. Sir Christopher Wren;

b. Grinling Gibbons;

c. Robert Adams;

d. John Nash.

5. In your notebook, write a paragraph about each of the following:

a. terraced town houses in the seventeenth and eighteenth centuries;

b. ribbon development;

c. council housing estates.

6. Try to visit an antique shop, a museum or a bric-a-brac stall on a market. Look at the old, everyday household articles and items of furniture on show. Choose two items which you think are interesting and make rough sketches of them. Find out what they are.

7. Look at the picture of nineteenth century workers' houses in Burnley. Make a list of the disadvantages of living in a back-to-back house.

AEROFILMS LTD

8. Imagine that you are wanting to buy a house. Where would you go to find out about property for sale? Make a list of the points you would consider when choosing where to live.

9. What are the advantages of:

a. prefabricated building methods;

b. medium-rise blocks of flats;

c. home insulation?

10. Walk round the streets near your home and make a list of the different:

a. types of housing you notice;

b. building materials used;

c. decorative features on the exteriors of houses.

Interior design or decoration

Interior design is the art of arranging furniture against an interesting background of colour, pattern and texture, so that homes become comfortable, efficient and pleasing places in which to live.

When planning interior design schemes there are several important points to consider.

1 The architectural character of the building

Does it lend itself to traditional furniture arranged in a formal setting or modern, simple units set in a bright, colourful, decorative scheme?

2 The shape and size of the room

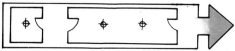

Is the room large or small? Has it a high or low ceiling?

3 The activities for which the room will be used

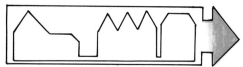

These will affect the colour scheme, the type of furnishings and the "mood" of the room, e.g. a living room should be a warm, comfortable and relaxing room, whereas a bedroom needs to be cool and restful.

4 The aspect of the room

Do the windows face north or south? Is the room naturally light and warm, or dark and cold? Is there a pleasant view from the windows?

5 The focal feature of the room

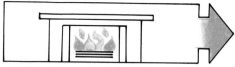

This may be an impressive fireplace, large windows, an eye-catching painting or an existing major furnishing item, such as a carpet or seating arrangement. If there is a feature that the eye is drawn to immediately, it is a good idea to build a design scheme around this.

6 The likes and dislikes of the occupants

Although ideas can be copied from magazines, exhibitions and other people's homes, interior design should reflect the personalities and the personal preferences of the people living in the house.

It is important to consider each of these points when planning interior decoration but it is still possible to make mistakes. Not everybody has the flair or confidence to experiment with personal colour schemes, and if the finished result is not pleasing it can prove a costly mistake. Here are some rules or guidelines to help the inexperienced home decorator understand the value of colour, pattern and texture in interior design.

Colour

Colour can create or destroy a room. When used wisely it can be a magical, exciting ingredient which is capable of producing different effects. Colour can make a room look warm and inviting, or cool and restful. It can conjure up a soft and simple mood, or a stunning and dramatic effect.

When a ray of sunlight is passed through a glass prism, the light separates into different colours.

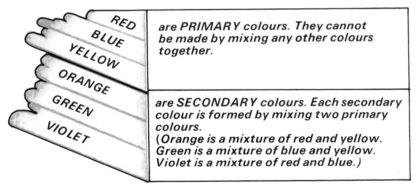

RED
BLUE
YELLOW

are PRIMARY colours. They cannot be made by mixing any other colours together.

ORANGE
GREEN
VIOLET

are SECONDARY colours. Each secondary colour is formed by mixing two primary colours.
(Orange is a mixture of red and yellow. Green is a mixture of blue and yellow. Violet is a mixture of red and blue.)

Where the primary and secondary colours overlap in a colour wheel, six new colours are formed. These are called **tertiary** colours. Try to look at a colour wheel in your art class, or prepare your own using paints or felt tip pens.

You will notice that opposite colours are in direct contrast to each other, e.g. red/green, blue/orange, yellow/violet. These are called **complementary** colours. Complementary colours create an intense, stimulating and dramatic effect, and they are not suitable for living areas or bedrooms where they could be irritating and restless. A complementary colour scheme could be used in halls, stairways and landings, or in rooms which are used for short periods of time, e.g.

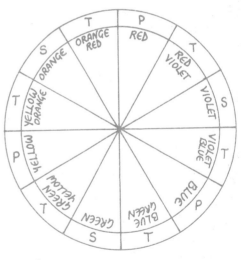

KEY

P	PRIMARY COLOURS
S	SECONDARY COLOURS
T	TERTIARY COLOURS

dining rooms. Here the stimulating effect would not be too overpowering. Adjacent colours on the colour wheel are **harmonious** colours, and produce a restful, tranquil atmosphere. A harmonious colour scheme is suitable for living areas and bedrooms. It is sometimes helpful to enliven a harmonious colour scheme with the addition of a single contrasting colour used in small amounts, e.g. on scatter cushions, lampshades, paintings, rugs or ornaments.

Black, white and grey are neutral colours because they blend or mix with complementary and harmonious colours. When black is added to a **hue** (colour), a **shade** is formed. When white is added to a hue, a **tint** is produced. The degree of darkness or lightness in a shade or tint is described as the **tone** of a colour. A wide range of tonal variety can be produced by the addition of white through grey to black. When black is used in a colour scheme it absorbs light, making adjacent colours seem brighter. For this reason small patches of black are often used successfully as accessories in a room. Dark grey has the same intensifying effect on adjacent colours. White reflects light and so makes other colours seem less brilliant. It helps to link or merge strong colours, and is effective on woodwork such as doors, window frames and skirting boards. Light grey produces the same softening effect on adjacent colours.

Some colours are warm and inviting. Reds, pinks and autumnal shades of brown are warm, close colours. Red is a colour which is associated with danger. It reminds the brain of fire and blood and makes a person alert, raising the pulse and blood pressure. It is therefore an excellent colour for "danger" signs such as road signs, traffic light signals, the red flag displayed on beaches when swimming is dangerous, etc. When warm colours are used in large amounts they are **advancing** colours, making a room look smaller. A high ceiling will appear to be lower if painted in a warm, dark colour. Large rooms will look smaller and more intimate if the walls are decorated in an advancing colour to reduce the apparent size of the room.

Light, pale colours, such as cream, pale yellow, pale blue, pale green are cool, remote colours. Blue is a colour which is associated with the sky and water. It is therefore a cool and

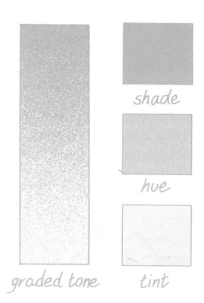

shade

hue

tint

graded tone

refreshing colour. It can have a soothing, restful quality, lowering the pulse and blood pressure. When cool colours are used in large amounts they are **receding** colours, giving an airy, spacious feeling and making walls and ceilings appear to move further away. Small dark rooms can be made to look bigger and lighter by using pale colours in the decorating scheme, and a low ceiling will appear higher if painted in a cool, receding colour.

This illustrates how easy it is to change the apparent shape and size of a room by the clever use of colour. Look at the room illustrated. It is long and narrow. By using a warm colour on the end walls (to bring them inwards) and a cool colour on the longer walls (to push them outwards), the illusion of a better proportioned room can be created.

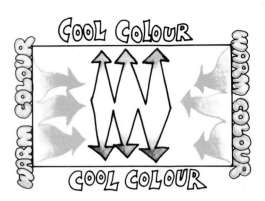

The choice of a colour scheme should be influenced by the aspect or location of a room. A north facing room will be cool, therefore a warm colour scheme will help to compensate for the natural coolness. A south facing room will have bright sunlight for most of the day, so a cooler scheme will be refreshing, helping to tone down the intensity of the natural light. If a room faces east it will get the early morning sun but will be in shade for the rest of the day, and if a room faces west it will be in shade during the morning but will get the afternoon sun. When planning a colour scheme for such rooms, it is important to consider the time of day when the room is used most. If a room is used when there is little or no natural sunlight, a warm colour scheme will be more pleasant than a cold one.

When planning a colour scheme it is helpful to divide a room into three separate parts.

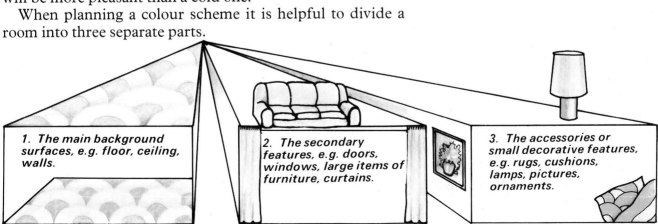

1. The main background surfaces, e.g. floor, ceiling, walls.

2. The secondary features, e.g. doors, windows, large items of furniture, curtains.

3. The accessories or small decorative features, e.g. rugs, cushions, lamps, pictures, ornaments.

A safe colour scheme can be evolved by choosing the main or dominant colour for the secondary areas, and having the large background areas in a light, neutral colour. Accessories can then be picked out in harmonious or complementary colours depending on the effect required. In very large rooms it is possible to use the dominant colour of a scheme for the main background surfaces, and a neutral colour for the secondary features. Harmonious or complementary accessories can be added as desired.

Pattern

If only plain colours are used in a decorative scheme the result will be bare and monotonous. The eye needs contrast, or some point it can focus upon to give relief from plain and empty spaces. This is where pattern is important. Pattern is used to break up plain areas and give interest and visual excitement to the eye. It also allows the eye to pause and relax momentarily whilst it takes in all the details.

It is important to use pattern sparingly. Too much pattern in a room is confusing and irritating to the eyes. Here are some points you should remember when choosing patterns for a room.

1 The motif or size of pattern should be in proportion to the area to be covered. For example, a small room needs a small repeat pattern, whereas a large room can happily take a large design.

2 Do not have too many different patterned surfaces in any one room. The different patterns will compete with each other and confuse and irritate the eye, and no one pattern will be seen at its best. The golden rule is to choose pattern carefully and to keep it to a minimum.

3 A bold, large pattern stands out, appearing closer than it actually is. In a large room, therefore, a bold repeat pattern can be used effectively to reduce the apparent size of the area.

4 The aim when decorating small modern rooms is to give an illusion of space. Neat geometrical repeat patterns are ideal for curtains. When used with plain or textured walls they appear to push the walls outwards, creating more space and light. This is illustrated in the picture.

This pattern is too big for the area to be covered. It cannot be seen properly because there is not enough space for pattern repeats.

A suitable decorative scheme for a small bedroom.

5 It is often safer to choose one patterned area for a room, and to set it against a background of plain or textured surfaces. Here are three ways of doing this in a living room.

1. A patterned carpet with plain and textured walls, furniture and curtains.

2. Patterned curtains with plain and textured walls, carpet and furniture.

3. Patterned upholstered furniture with plain and textured walls, carpet and curtains.

6 If a second pattern is introduced into a room, it should be smaller, neater and more restrained than the dominant pattern, so that it doesn't compete with the main pattern or spoil its effect. Ideally, a second pattern should be placed at a distance from the main patterned area, not adjacent to it. In this way the eye can travel from one pattern across a restful plain surface before it comes to the second pattern.

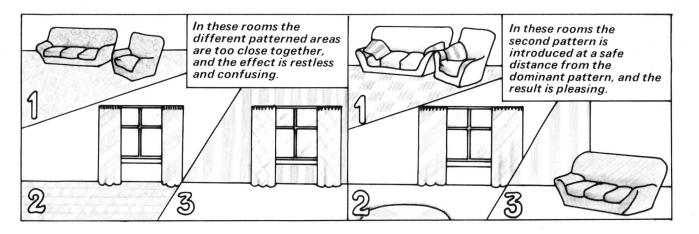

In these rooms the different patterned areas are too close together, and the effect is restless and confusing.

In these rooms the second pattern is introduced at a safe distance from the dominant pattern, and the result is pleasing.

7 Sometimes an identical pattern can be used on different surfaces, e.g.:

matching curtains and bedspread

matching curtains and cushion covers

matching curtains and wall covering

matching blinds and wall covering

This can look pleasing, especially if the two patterned surfaces are separated by plain or textured areas. When matching patterned surfaces are used in this way in a small room, it is important to choose the pattern carefully. A neat, small motif may be effective, but a strong repeat pattern could be disastrous.

8 When two different patterns are used in a room they should be linked in some particular way, e.g. matching colours or a similarity of motif. Here the bold pattern of the settee is echoed in the cushion covers and curtains.

9 A pattern should suit the particular surface for which it is being used. A wallpaper design should lie flat against the wall and not have a three-dimensional effect which "springs out" of the wall to meet you. Similarly, a patterned carpet should lie flat on the floor. Be wary of bold geometrical repeat patterns on carpets unless you have actually seen a large carpeted area. "Op art" patterns can sometimes play tricks on the eyes, appearing to move about and become distorted. Patterned curtains should look as effective opened as closed, and should always drape well. Upholstery fabrics should suit the shape or contours of the furniture. Check that patterns with a large motif are placed symmetrically, i.e. the two halves of the chair should match.

The two halves of this chair do NOT match because the large motif has been placed off-centre.

This chair looks "balanced".

10 Patterns can affect the shape and mood of a room in the same way that colours can.

    a Vertical stripes appear to raise the ceiling, increasing the height of a room.

    b Horizontal stripes appear to extend the walls, making a room look wider.

    c Diagonal and zig-zag patterns have a restless quality. They are eye-catching and dynamic.

    d Curves are soothing and restful.

    e Strong, bold patterns make a room look smaller.

This illustrates how easy it is to change the apparent shape and size of a room by the clever use of pattern. Look at this room. It is long and narrow. By using a strong pattern on the end walls (to bring them inwards) and a plain or textured surface on the longer walls (to push them outwards), the illusion of a better proportioned room can be created quite easily.

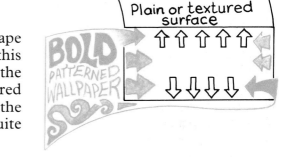

Texture

Run your hand lightly over the furnishings and furniture near you, and feel the variety of different surfaces. Some feel soft and warm. Others are cold and shiny. Feel the different degrees of roughness or smoothness. The "feel" of a surface is called its texture.

    Texture plays an important part in interior decoration. It gives interest to surfaces but unlike pattern it does not irritate or confuse the eye. Texture helps to create a mood without reducing the apparent size of a room. A variety of different textured surfaces adds appeal, and a combination of harmonious and contrasting textures gives a pleasing effect to any decorative scheme. Look at pictures of living rooms and notice the different textured surfaces, e.g. rough tweed upholstery, solid pine furniture, glazed earthenware tiles, smooth short-piled carpets, silky long-piled rugs, dry crisp grasses, plain painted chimney breast, wallpaper, brass cupboard knobs, softly draping curtains. From the pictures, list some other textured surfaces which help to create an attractive room.

    Here are some points to remember when using texture in interior decoration.

1 Texture can bring a dull, unimaginative area to life. When paint is applied to a flat surface such as a plastered wall, the effect can be lifeless. If the same paint is put on a textured wall, e.g. rough brick, stippled plaster, "woodchip" or Anaglypta wallpaper, the effect is completely different. The wall becomes interesting and pleasing to the eye.

2 Texture alters the appearance of colour. A rough texture absorbs light making a surface look darker, but a smooth texture reflects light producing a lighter effect. If the same colour is painted on adjacent walls which have contrasting textures, the smooth wall will look lighter than the rough wall. This principle can be used to good effect when decorating a room. Rough surfaces can be used to highlight special features such as chimney breasts and alcoves, and smooth surfaces can be used to lighten dark areas.

3 Textured walls and ceilings create an illusion of space by seeming to push the surfaces outwards.

4 A textured wall covering can be used to cover flaws and cracks in walls, and to disguise uneven or irregular surfaces. This is an important point to remember when decorating old buildings.

5 The clever use of texture can influence the mood of a room. Plain, smooth, silk-like surfaces create a feeling of elegance, formality and richness, whereas chunky, rough materials produce a cosy, casual and comfortable mood which seems homely and relaxing.

This room has an air of elegance and formality.

This room seems cosy and comfortable.

6 Every room should have some variety of texture. A room consisting of even-textured surfaces is boring and un-interesting. Texture and interest can be added by the simple use of a shaggy rug, tweed-covered scatter cushions, a chunky lamp base or an unusual shade.

7 Deep-pile carpeting gives a warm feeling and may be more suited to a cool room than one which has a sunny southern aspect. For the same reason, smooth carpeting is often more successful in warm rooms. It can create a depressingly icy effect when used in cool rooms.

Quality of materials

When planning any decorative scheme, always choose good quality materials. A well-known reputable brand of paint may not be the cheapest available, but it should:

have a good appearance when dry

last well and retain its colour and surface even after cleaning

be easy to use

Similarly, a good quality wallpaper will be a sound investment. It should:

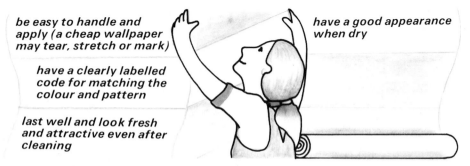

be easy to handle and apply (a cheap wallpaper may tear, stretch or mark)

have a clearly labelled code for matching the colour and pattern

last well and look fresh and attractive even after cleaning

have a good appearance when dry

There is a wide selection of wall, floor and ceiling coverings available for the home decorator and here are some of the materials currently in the shops.

Wall coverings

Most interior wall surfaces are of smooth plaster. It can be:

   a   painted;
   b   covered in a variety of different wallpaper finishes;
   c   tiled;
   d   covered in wood panelling;
   e   covered in fabrics e.g. woven grass cloth, hessian, silk;
   f   covered in vinyl plastic wall covering;
   g   covered in polystyrene sheeting.

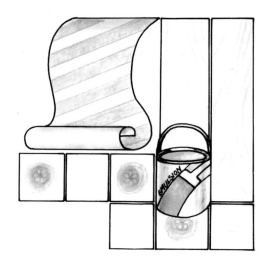

Paint

Paint gives a relatively inexpensive finish which is easy to apply and lasts well. There is the added advantage that a painted wall can be readily changed to match a new colour scheme, when necessary. Here is a chart showing the different types of paint and where each one can be used.

Type of paint	Advantages/Disadvantages	Where suitable
Alkyd resin or gloss (an oil-based paint which may have a high gloss, semi-gloss, sheen or matt finish)	Easy to clean. Tougher than water-based paints but takes longer to dry. Some people find the smell unpleasant when the paint is drying.	Used for woodwork (doors, windows, skirting boards, staircases).
Acrylic (a water-based paint which may have vinyl or polyurethane added to make it tougher. Matt, silk or satin)	Dries quickly. Shiny finished acrylics can show brush marks. Very little smell.	Can be used on plastered surfaces (walls, ceilings) and on woodwork.
Emulsion (a water-based paint which has a matt finish)	Dries quickly. Does not leave brush marks. Has no unpleasant smell.	Suitable for plastered surfaces or painting over textured wallpapers.
Thixotropic (a gloss or emulsion paint in a gel-like form)	Spreads easily but cannot be brushed out to a fine finish. Does not drip from brush. One coat may be sufficient.	Can be used on plastered surfaces and on woodwork.

Wallpaper

Wallpaper can transform a room giving it warmth and personality but care must be taken to choose a wallpaper that has the right colour, texture and pattern to produce the effect required. There are four main types of domestic wallpaper and it is important to know for which surfaces and rooms each one is suitable. Here is a chart which should act as a guide.

Type of wallpaper	Advantages/Disadvantages	Where suitable
Ordinary (has a pattern printed on to single or double thickness paper)	Cannot be washed clean so marks and stains show.	Living rooms and bedrooms. Not suitable for areas where it may get dirty quickly, or for "damp" places such as bathrooms and kitchens.
Wipeable or washable (has a thin protective film covering the paper)	Can be wiped or washed with a damp cloth.	Bathrooms and kitchens.
Vinyl	More expensive than ordinary wallpaper but is easy to cut and handle. Not marked by water or paste, and slides on wall surface making pattern matching easy. When stripping, vinyl sheet lifts away from backing paper which can be left on wall. Very hard wearing and can be scrubbed clean.	Can be used in any area of the home.
Embossed, e.g. Anaglypta, Supaglypta, Vynaglypta (Lincrusta is a very heavily embossed wall covering which is permanent)	Hides surfaces which are uneven. Gives texture to walls. Provides a tough covering which can be painted over and over again.	Ceilings and walls in any area of the home.

"Woodchip" paper has wooden chips sandwiched between two layers of paper. It is a hard-wearing paper with a rough textured surface which looks well on feature walls, chimney breasts or alcoves, but should not be used in large quantities.

There are three ways of applying wallpaper and the correct method is indicated on each roll.

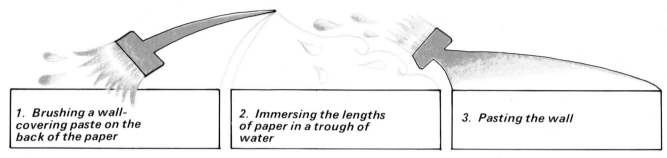

1. Brushing a wall-covering paste on the back of the paper

2. Immersing the lengths of paper in a trough of water

3. Pasting the wall

Tiles

Wall tiling gives an attractive and permanent finish but may look hard and impersonal if used over large areas. Wall tiles can be used for:

   a functional areas such as around sinks, baths, showers etc.;

   b small decorative arrangements;

   c feature walls.

Here are some tiles which are suitable for wall surfaces.

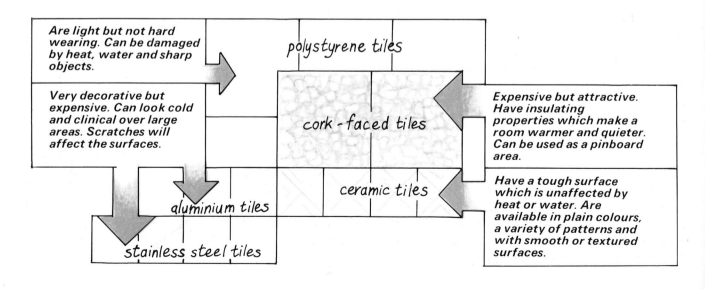

Are light but not hard wearing. Can be damaged by heat, water and sharp objects.

Very decorative but expensive. Can look cold and clinical over large areas. Scratches will affect the surfaces.

polystyrene tiles

cork-faced tiles

aluminium tiles

ceramic tiles

stainless steel tiles

Expensive but attractive. Have insulating properties which make a room warmer and quieter. Can be used as a pinboard area.

Have a tough surface which is unaffected by heat or water. Are available in plain colours, a variety of patterns and with smooth or textured surfaces.

Wood panelling

Wood panelling is an attractive, permanent wall covering which can be stuck directly to plaster with a special adhesive, or pinned to wooden battens at regular intervals. It can be used on individual feature walls or on every wall in a room. Wood panelling used vertically appears either to add height to a wall or decrease the length of a room, and used horizontally it either increases the length of a room or lowers the ceiling.

Dark wood looks dignified and warm, and goes well with traditional-type furniture, though it may be oppressive in a small room. Light-coloured wood looks fresh and homely, and blends with modern units or chunky pine furniture.

Solid wood panelling is expensive but it has good insulation properties and makes a cold room warmer. It can be sealed to give a hard-wearing finish which is easy to clean. Individual planks or boards can also be used. These are stained and sealed to enhance their natural grain pattern and knots. A cheaper form of wood panelling consists of thin plywood sheets which are covered with a veneer of good-quality wood.

It is wise to treat all timber walls with a fire-retardant paint.

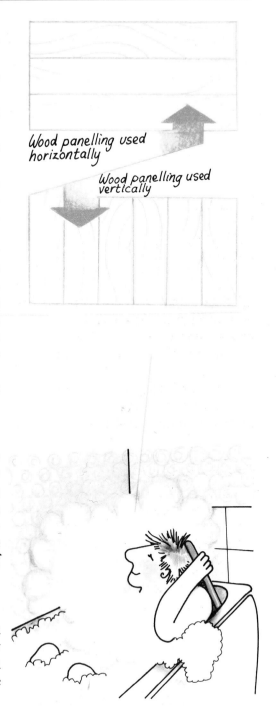

Wood panelling used horizontally

Wood panelling used vertically

Fabric coverings

Fabrics such as hessian, grass cloth and silk make attractive textured coverings for feature walls, but they are very expensive and do not wear well. Panels of hessian and grass cloth cannot be matched so the seams are noticeable. When hanging fabric coverings it is important to allow for shrinkage as they dry out. Silk is luxurious but has a delicate surface which will not stand up well to the wear and tear of everyday life.

Vinyl plastic

Vinyl plastic wall coverings are available in sheet form in a variety of colours, patterns and textures. They are extremely hard wearing and are unaffected by moisture, making them ideal for bathrooms and kitchens. Some designs are suitable for living rooms and bedrooms.

Polystyrene sheeting

Expanded polystyrene is a light textured material which can be hung like sheets of wallpaper. It helps to insulate a room against heat loss and damp, and has some sound-proofing properties. This type of wall surface, however, is inflammable. To reduce the fire risk:

a choose a self-extinguishing grade of expanded polystyrene;

b paint with an emulsion paint (***never*** an oil-based gloss) or

c use a fire-retardant paint.

Polystyrene is not a durable wall covering. It will be damaged by knocks, scratches and abrasions.

Floor coverings

Most floor surfaces in a home are of wood or concrete. If the original timber floor is in good condition, it can be sanded and sealed to make a natural wood floor which looks beautiful anywhere. If this is not possible, the floorboards can be covered with another material. Concrete is too hard and cold to leave as it is, so this surface is nearly always covered.

There are many floor coverings which can be laid on wood or concrete. Here are some:

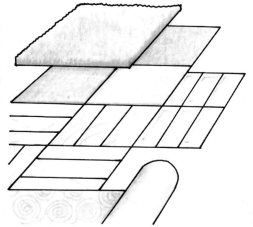

a carpet;

b tiles or brick;

c vinyl, linoleuin, or cork in sheet form;

d wood.

Carpet

A carpet gives a feeling of warmth and comfort. It muffles sounds, helps to insulate against draughts and provides a non-slip easy-to-clean surface. Carpet can be bought as:

a wall-to-wall or fitted carpeting;

b carpet squares;

c scatter rugs;

d carpet tiles.

Try to suggest some advantages and disadvantages for each of these.

There are three main types of carpet as shown in the illustration at the top of page 37.

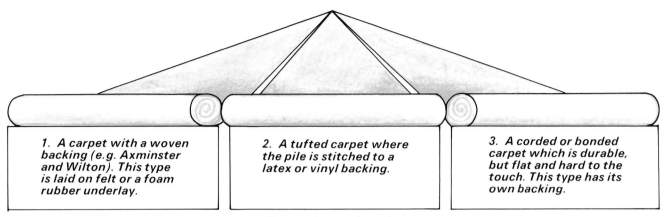

1. *A carpet with a woven backing (e.g. Axminster and Wilton). This type is laid on felt or a foam rubber underlay.*

2. *A tufted carpet where the pile is stitched to a latex or vinyl backing.*

3. *A corded or bonded carpet which is durable, but flat and hard to the touch. This type has its own backing.*

Here are some points to remember when choosing carpeting.

1 Carpeting is graded to suit particular areas in the home and is usually labelled for light, medium or heavy usage. Always check that the carpet you choose is the right quality for the type of wear it is likely to get.

2 Buy the best you can afford. It is a good idea to choose a reputable brand and to ask for expert advice.

3 Remember to select colour, pattern and texture sensibly.

Tiles or brick

Earthenware or ceramic tiles are expensive to install but they make an attractive permanent floor covering which is suitable for bathrooms, dining rooms, hallways and terraces. They are available in plain colours, a variety of patterns and with smoothly glazed or roughly textured surfaces.

Vinyl, linoleum or cork tiles are cheaper. They are warmer, more comfortable to the feet and less noisy than ceramic tiles. They are not a permanent covering and can be removed if necessary. Vinyl and linoleum are both hard-wearing materials. Cushioned vinyl has a built-in underlay and is soft and warm to the feet. Cork is soft and quiet underfoot, and has insulating properties. It may, however, need to be varnished for protection.

Polished brick can be used in hallways and terraces. It forms an attractive floor covering but is difficult to maintain in good condition. The surface scratches easily, and the sealing and waxing necessary for protection makes the

surface slippery when wet. Brick is therefore not suitable for kitchens and bathrooms.

Vinyl, linoleum, or cork in sheet form

Vinyl sheet floor coverings are flexible and hard wearing. They can be obtained in a variety of colours and patterns, and with smooth or textured surfaces. They do not show stains and are easy to keep clean. Cushioned vinyls are warm and soft to the touch. Vinyl floors are suitable for kitchens, bathrooms, hallways and children's rooms.

Linoleum is hard wearing but not as comfortable or as easy to clean as cushioned vinyl. It is available in a limited number of colours and patterns.

Cork looks and feels warm. It is quiet and soft underfoot but can be damaged by sharp objects. Its insulation properties make it suitable for children's rooms.

Wood

Wooden floors can range from simple pine floorboards to elegant parquet and block mosaic floors. Wood is a hard-wearing material which gives a warm, rich effect to a room. An old wooden floor can be sanded and sealed or sanded and painted. A new wooden floor is expensive to buy but gives a permanent floor covering which should last a lifetime. Many different woods can be used, and a variety of patterns can be built up from wooden blocks, parquet squares or strips of wood.

Wood can become slippery when wet or highly polished, so it is not a suitable floor covering for kitchens, bathrooms or hallways.

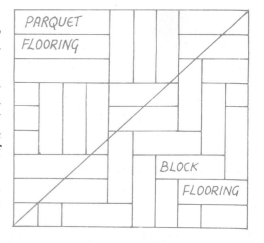

Ceiling coverings

The ceiling surface is usually of plasterboard or plaster. It is important to start with a smooth surface when decorating ceilings, so do check that the plaster is in good condition and that cracks have been filled in.

There are several types of ceiling covering. The most usual being:

a paint;

b paper and paint;

c polystyrene sheeting or tiles;
d textured stippling;
e wood.

Paint

If the surface of a ceiling is in good condition, it can be painted directly. White, off white or restrained neutral colours are popular, but remember that colour can influence the apparent height of a ceiling, so choose a colour which suits the room. A dramatic way to "lower" a high ceiling is to paint it in a dark colour and use electric light fittings to direct the light downwards. A pleasant effect can be obtained by painting the ceiling to match the walls or by using a pale tint of the dominant colour in the decorative scheme. Another idea which is quite effective is to paint the ceiling to link up with or echo the main colour of the floor, leaving the walls neutral.

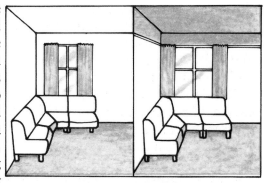

Paper and paint

A ceiling should be papered before being painted if the plaster is cracked or irregular, or the joins between plasterboards show. The paper can be a smooth lining paper or one of the textured finishes such as Anaglypta, Supaglypta, Vynaglypta or Lincrusta. If the ceiling surface is very poor, it helps to "cross line", by pasting smooth lining paper in one direction and a textured paper on the top going at right angles to the lining paper. When the ceiling paper has dried it can be painted the required colour.

Polystyrene sheeting or tiles

Expanded polystyrene can be hung like sheets of ceiling paper or stuck to a ceiling as individual tiles. If individual tiles are being used, it is easier to paint the tiles before fixing them to the ceiling. Remember that polystyrene is inflammable. To reduce the fire risk, see page 36.

Textured stippling

Textured stippling is a permanent ceiling covering which can be used to disguise very rough plaster. The thick decorative compound is brushed on the ceiling, a small area at a time, and then given a textured finish with a roller or sponge.

Wood

A timbered ceiling is a permanent surface which looks attractive, rich and warm. Wooden boards can be laid on top of the plaster and fixed to the joists, or the plaster ceiling can be removed altogether. A polyurethane seal or stain can be applied to enhance the grain and knots in the wood. Exposed beams blend with the character of old buildings, and should be retained as a special decorative feature whenever possible. They look very effective when set against a plain white ceiling.

A word about cove cornices

Cove cornices are curved strips of material which are used to cover the join between walls and ceiling. They form a permanent edge which can be painted to match the walls or ceiling, or picked out in a contrasting colour. They can be made of expanded polystyrene strips or of gypsum plaster.

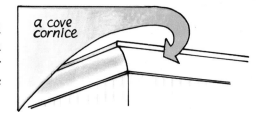

a cove cornice

Staircases

Unless a house is being built to your own design it is not usually possible to alter the position or type of staircase because it will have been designed as a structural feature of the house. It is possible, though, to disguise an unattractive staircase by clever interior decoration. Here are some helpful points.

1 Treat the hall, stairs and landing areas as one, making the colour scheme continuous, leading upwards via the staircase. When the same wall, floor and ceiling coverings are used, an illusion of space is created, an important point to remember when decorating modern houses where space may be limited.

2 If the staircase is steep and narrow, a light bright colour scheme will help. Avoid large patterns in floor or wall coverings and rely on texture or tiny repeat patterns to push the walls outwards. A carpet with a horizontal stripe will widen a narrow staircase.

3 The wall of a half-open staircase can be made a feature wall. You may choose to:

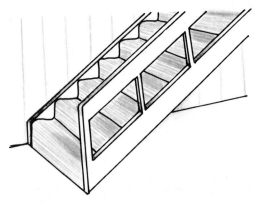

a use a distinctive wallpaper;

b arrange pictures and paintings against a plain background;

c cover the wall with wood panelling;

d use mirrors or mirror tiles to "double" the area.

4 If the banister is filled in, this creates a barrier between the staircase and the hall and landing. Try linking these areas by removing the hardboard panelling and leaving just a handrail. If there are young children in the house, a handrail will not be sufficient to stop them falling through the open stairway, so insert open wrought iron railings or simple wooden strips. The hall and landing can then be seen through the staircase, making the whole area seem larger.

5 See that the stairs are well lit. Ceiling and pendant fittings are suitable but check that they do not glare or cast shadows. Wall fittings are not easy to position on a staircase. If they are too high, cleaning and changing bulbs becomes dangerous, and if lights are too low they may be knocked down. A group of pendant lights suspended at different heights makes an attractive feature.

Windows

A window lets in light and air. When there is also an attractive view, this is an added bonus, and the window covering should be used to enhance the effect. If the view is unattractive, it can be hidden or disguised by choosing a suitable covering. When the decorative scheme of a room is planned, the window covering should be chosen to blend in with the colour, pattern and texture of the other furnishings. It should help to reflect the mood. This may be homely and informal, traditional or very modern.

There are several different types of window covering. The most usual ones are:

a curtains;

b blinds and shades;

c shutters.

Curtains

Curtains can be long or short. They can hang loosely or drape elaborately to frame the window. They can be suspended from neat-looking tracks or from decorative poles. Pelmets and valances may be used at the top of the windows, or the curtains can be made with pleated headings which are decorative features in themselves.

Long curtains help to exclude draughts from badly-fitting window frames and this is worth remembering when furnishing old houses. When covering the windows of a double-glazed modern house, the only points to consider are decoration, privacy and controlling any glare from the sun. Very full curtains in a light and transparent fabric may be the answer. Net or sheer curtains hung close to the window glass give privacy during the daytime, and can be teamed with opaque draw curtains which can be closed at night. Café curtains are hung on rods. They may cover the lower half of the window or be arranged in overlapping tiers. Café curtains can be used to hide an unattractive view or to give privacy, without blocking out all the sunlight.

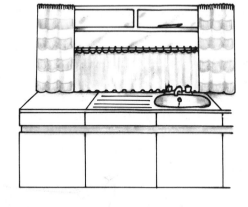

Curtains can improve the look of badly shaped or positioned windows. Narrow windows can be widened by extending the curtains at either side of the window frame, and floor length curtains will improve the appearance of small windows. Horizontally striped curtains will make narrow windows look wider and vertically striped curtains will make short widish windows seem taller. Where two windows are on the same wall, the curtaining can be extended to cover both windows. An attractive treatment for double windows is to curtain the entire wall, giving the illusion of a large picture window.

Here are some pictures showing curtaining used in different ways.

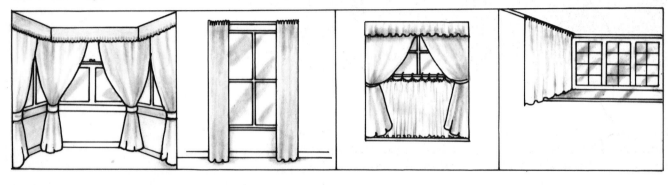

Blinds and shades

Blinds can be used alone or they can be combined with curtains. Venetian blinds are hard wearing and are made of horizontal aluminium or plastic strips which can be lifted or dropped as required. Roller blinds are less expensive. They can be bought in plain colours or in a variety of attractive patterns. Some have decorative trimmings and pull-cords attached. Roller blinds can be made to order or they can be purchased as "do-it-yourself" kits. It is possible to buy matching roller blinds, curtains and wallpapers and these can look very effective. The slatted louvred curtain has become fashionable. This type can be adjusted so that the required amount of sunlight or privacy is obtained.

Roman shades draw upwards folding like a concertina, making them look attractive at the window even when pulled up.

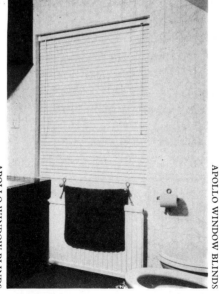

A louvred curtain   A venetian blind

Shutters

Solid or louvred shutters can be made to fit almost any window. The wood can be varnished or painted a gay colour to match the decorative scheme of the room. They look attractive both closed and open, and they are ideal for ensuring privacy. Shutters can be combined with curtains or they can be used by themselves. Highly ornate and decorative shutters can be made of vinyl or metal, with cane or fabric covering stretched between the supports.

Doors

Doors in modern houses are often made of plain hardboard which is painted white or a neutral colour to match the other woodwork in the room. If the door is positioned well, why not paint it in a gay colour and decorate it with an attractive knob and finger plate? The panels of a panelled door can be picked out in a different colour, or the whole surface can be painted with an attractive wood finish.

A louvred door looks different, and the three-quarter length "ranch-style" door can make an interesting feature linking two rooms.

Ideas for fireplaces

A fireplace can be the hub of family life. It makes an attractive focal point of a room. Paintings, photographs and mirrors can be hung above it, and favourite ornaments can be displayed on the mantle. Seating units can be grouped around it, and comfortable shaggy rugs arranged by the hearth.

If an existing fireplace looks plain and unimaginative, try covering it with new tiles or build an extended stone hearth to add interest. This can provide space for potted plants, a store of chopped logs and comfortable seating cushions. A timbered, brick or stone wall makes an effective background for an open fire.

Many modern homes are built without fireplaces. Some are centrally heated and others have gas or electric wall fires with elegant surrounds of wood or metal. In Chapter Four we shall discuss the various ways of heating a home, and how to choose well-designed heating appliances.

louvred door

Think and Do

1. Name the following:

a. a primary colour;

b. a secondary colour;

c. a tertiary colour;

d. a warm, advancing colour;

e. a cold, receding colour;

f. a neutral colour.

2. With the aid of diagrams say how you would:

a. add interest to a dull, unimaginative fireplace;

b. make a narrow window look wider;

c. "push out" the walls of a small dark room;

d. "lift" a low ceiling;

e. use pattern or texture to highlight a feature wall in a living room.

3. Draw and colour a design for a kitchen or bathroom wallpaper.

4. Write a few sentences about each of the following:

a. cove cornices;

b. embossed wallpapers;

c. polystyrene tiles;

d. thixotropic paint;

e. wood panelling.

5. Try to find *ten* wall coverings which are hidden in this word maze. They may be written horizontally, vertically, diagonally or backwards.

6. What is the difference between:

a. venetian and roller blinds;

b. a harmonious and a complementary colour scheme;

c. an oil-based and a water-based paint;

d. pattern and texture?

7. Look at the diagrams overleaf. Using a decorator's colour chart, suggest a suitable colour scheme for each of the areas shown. Say how you would use pattern and texture to add interest to each room.

P	I	H	C	D	O	O	W	A	S
O	N	L	M	E	S	C	T	K	B
W	A	L	L	P	A	P	E	R	W
F	E	I	K	T	Y	W	O	O	D
L	P	J	S	L	A	G	S	C	K
T	A	O	G	H	I	R	E	T	L
S	I	A	E	B	Y	S	L	U	W
I	N	M	H	E	S	S	I	A	N
A	T	C	O	R	V	E	T	O	B
D	A	T	S	U	R	C	N	I	L

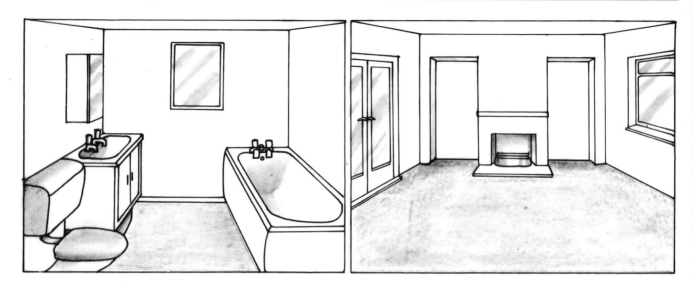

8. Copy out the following crossword and complete it.

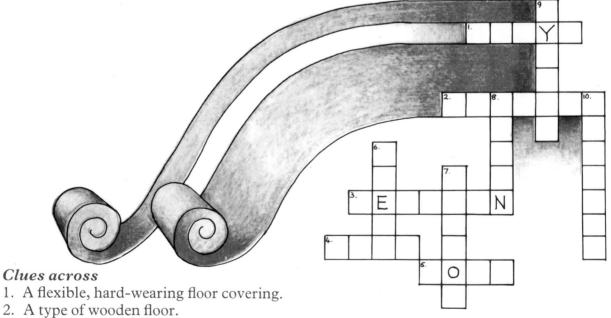

Clues across
1. A flexible, hard-wearing floor covering.
2. A type of wooden floor.
3. A fabric wall covering.
4. This is produced when white is added to a colour.
5. A soft floor or wall covering which has insulation properties.

Clues down

6. A secondary colour.
7. A carpet with a woven backing.
8. This type of shade draws upwards like a concertina.
9 Cove cornices can be made of this.
10. This describes the "feel" of a surface.

9. Suggest a suitable covering for:

a. a bathroom wall;
b. a kitchen floor;
c. a staircase wall;
d. a living room ceiling where the plaster has cracked;
e. a double-glazed window with a southerly aspect;
f. a bedroom window on the ground floor;
g. a hall floor;
h. a feature wall in a child's playroom.

10. Why is it important to use good-quality materials when decorating? List some points to consider when choosing and using:

a. paint;
b. wallpaper.

Room planning

In the last chapter we saw the importance of colour, pattern, texture, style and quality of materials when decorating rooms. Now we shall look at the rooms of a house individually and consider the various activities associated with each one. When we have assessed the functions of a room, it is possible to plan work zones. A work zone is made by grouping together all the tools, equipment, storage space, appliances or furniture for any particular activity. This reduces movement to a minimum, saving time and energy.

The kitchen

The main activities involved in a kitchen are the **preparation and storage of food**, the **cooking and serving of food** and **washing up**. Unless there is a separate utility room, the kitchen will probably also have to house equipment for the **laundering of clothes**. If a family only uses the dining room area for "special occasion" meals, the kitchen may also be used for **eating**, and any toddlers or young children will use the kitchen as a **playing area** while their mothers are working there. Most of these activities require storage units, working surfaces and separate appliances.

In a well-planned kitchen each group of equipment is placed together to make convenient work zones. In a small or average-sized kitchen it is not always possible to completely segregate each activity because some tasks require an overlapping of equipment. The kitchen sink, for example, is needed for the preparation, cooking and serving of food, and for washing up, and it may also be needed when doing the family wash. In a large kitchen it is possible to separate each activity by creating:

    a a preparation/working/cooking zone;
    b an eating area;
    c a laundry section.

Travel to and from the equipment can be cut down by having island or peninsula units. An island unit can be used from all four sides and usually consists of a sink, cooker hob and working surface. The base of the island must be cut away so that it is possible to stand close to the unit. An island unit should have at least two power points. A peninsula unit creates two separate areas. One side of the divider can be used for storage cupboards, and the other side as a breakfast counter with bar stools or dining chairs.

An efficient kitchen layout has an unbroken working surface linking the cooker and the sink, with an additional worktop on the further sides of the appliances. The sequence is, therefore: worktop-cooker-worktop-sink-worktop, with no gaps or obstructions in between. The food storage unit or refrigerator should be conveniently placed to form a compact triangle.

It is important to ensure that there is no through traffic on the path from the sink to the cooker to cause a safety hazard. The actual size and shape of the kitchen will determine the position of the various items. They can be arranged in an L shape, a U shape or in a straight line.

An island unit

A peninsula unit

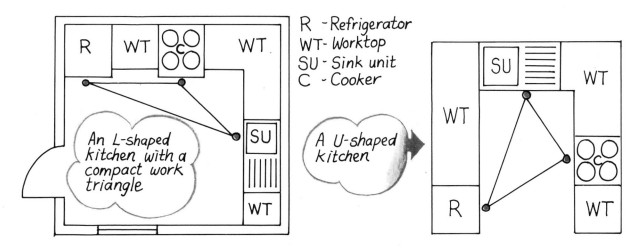

R - Refrigerator
WT - Worktop
SU - Sink unit
C - Cooker

An L-shaped kitchen with a compact work triangle

A U-shaped kitchen

Worktops should be at a convenient height. Base units can usually be lowered or raised by means of a plinth, and this should be recessed so that it is possible to stand right up to the unit. Wall-hung units can be fixed at the height which suits you best. Here are some recommended heights for an average-sized person.

Work surface and cooker hob	**850–1000 mm above floor**
Sink top	**900–1050 mm** ,, ,,
Bottom of wall unit	**1350 mm** ,, ,,
Highest shelf in wall unit	**1800 mm** ,, ,,
Top of wall unit	**1925–2250 mm** ,, ,,

It is a good idea to insert shallow shelves in the spaces between worktops and overhead cupboards. These can be useful for storing herbs, spices, seasonings, mugs, canisters etc.

Try to store tools and implements close to where they will be needed. Saucepans should be near the cooker; washing up equipment near the sink; crockery and cutlery halfway between the sink and the eating area and laundry equipment near the washing machine. It is dangerous to have storage shelves above the cooker. Base units with pull-out basket drawers are far more accessible than deep shelves, and there is a range of clever storage accessories which clip on to the insides of doors.

Worktops should be hard wearing and easy to clean, with curved front edges and raised backs. Laminated plastic is an ideal kitchen surface. It is important to see that the worktops on either side of the cooker are level with the hob. This prevents spillage when transferring saucepans to and fro. Some worktops have insets of different materials, e.g. a stainless steel heatproof surface next to the hob, a marble slab for rolling out pastry, a wooden chopping board.

Ideally there should be at least five electric power points in the kitchen. If two are used continually for the refrigerator and freezer, this leaves three sockets available for the electric kettle/electric frying pan/toaster/food mixer/dishwasher/iron/slow cooker/washing machine/tumble drier/microwave oven/waste-disposal unit/water storage heater. It is unlikely that more than three of these items will be in use at the same time. The kitchen is one room where floor power points are not sensible. Most electrical kitchen gadgets are used at worktop height, so it is more convenient to have the power points sited there. It is a good idea to have double sockets and to use the type which has warning lights to indicate when an appliance has not been switched off. If you are designing a kitchen from scratch, remember that power points and switches should not be placed near the sink.

Natural lighting is provided by windows, which should be as large as possible. If there is only a small window in a kitchen it can often be extended upwards to increase the natural light. Another way to increase the natural light is to have a glass panel inserted in the back door. Bungalows can have extra windows built in the roof, if required. If kitchen windows face south, it may be necessary to have blinds which can be adjusted to eliminate glare.

Many kitchens have one central ceiling light. This may give sufficient artificial light in a small kitchen but it also casts a person's shadow on surfaces and appliances. If there is only one light in a kitchen the best position is probably between the cooker and the sink unit. Ideally a kitchen should have extra artificial lighting at important points such as the main working surface, the sink and the cooker. Extra lights can be positioned on the ceiling, on wall brackets or on the underside of wall cupboards. A fluorescent strip or tube light is better than a filament lamp because it gives less shadow, but this type of light can be harsh and "cold". A good solution is to have a ceiling-mounted fluorescent tube for all-round light, with additional tungsten lighting at important places.

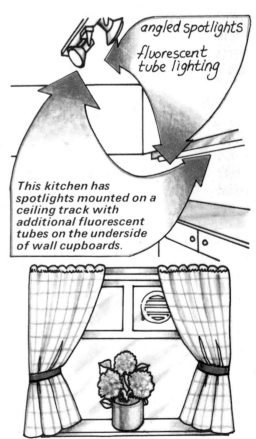

angled spotlights
fluorescent tube lighting

This kitchen has spotlights mounted on a ceiling track with additional fluorescent tubes on the underside of wall cupboards.

There should be good ventilation in a kitchen to disperse cooking smells, and the condensation caused by cooking, washing and drying activities. An open window will solve the problem in summer but will make the kitchen cold and draughty in winter. An extractor fan fitted in a window or on an outside wall is essential in a well-designed kitchen. The fan can be switched on whenever it is needed, and it does not cause any heat loss. There should also be some form of permanent ventilation, such as an air brick in a wall or an air grill in the door. This is particularly important if there are any gas appliances in the kitchen, e.g. a cooker or gas-fired central heating boiler. It is a good idea to have a wide hood over the cooker to trap steam and grease-laden fumes. The hood, which can have an attractive copper or stainless steel canopy usually has a duct to an outside wall and a ventilation fan to extract the food smells. If there is no duct to an outside wall, the hood can be fitted with a grease-trapping filter.

If a kitchen is very small, extra space can often be provided by moving some equipment elsewhere, e.g.:

1 The washing machine can be put in the bathroom, garage (if there is a sink) or utility room (if there is one).

2 The freezer can be moved to the garage or any suitable outhouse building (but, if so, choose a freezer with a locking mechanism).

3 The space under the stairs can be converted into a storage cupboard for equipment which is not used daily (vacuum cleaner, ironing board, tinned food).

4 If the dining room is used for all family meals, it will be more convenient to keep the eating and serving equipment there in a dresser or sideboard.

The bathroom

The bathroom is usually a small and purely functional room, which is designed for **washing**, **bathing** and **shaving** purposes. The **lavatory** is often included in the bathroom, but for practical and aesthetic reasons, a separate lavatory or an additional one is desirable. If the bathroom is fairly large it may also be used for **storage**. Enclosed cupboards and open shelves can be fitted above or around the bath and basin, or be tailored to fit any vacant floor space. Sliding cupboard doors take up less room than hinged opening doors. Cupboards and shelves can be used for storing toilet accessories: cleaning materials, clean towels, spare toilet rolls, cosmetics, first aid equipment, etc. (Medicines should be kept in a separate locked cabinet.)

The space above the bath makes useful hanging space for **drying** clothes. There are special drying rails which can be fixed over the bath, and a variety of pull-out clothes lines which can be attached to walls. Draped clothes can be hidden from view by an attractive screen.

Storage shelves above the bath

A downstairs bathroom may be used for *laundering* clothes. Hand washing can be done in the basin, and larger, bulkier items can be laundered in the bath. If there is room for a washing machine, it may make sense to put it in the bathroom, creating more space in the kitchen. It is a good idea to keep laundry equipment together, either in one corner of the bathroom, or fitted underneath a vanitory unit. If you intend using a bathroom for laundry equipment, do ask for expert advice about the siting and installation of appliances. There are safety hazards involved in using electrical equipment in the bathroom, and this means that the necessary power sockets and switches must be *outside* the room.

When planning a bathroom, always try to make the most of the space available. Position the various fittings so that there is enough room to use each item comfortably. The lavatory and bidet (if there is one) should be sited close to the basin for hygiene reasons. Any vacant spaces can then be fitted with storage units.

Washing and bathing equipment usually consists of a bath and/or shower unit, and a hand basin. If the size and shape of the room allow, there may also be a bidet but this is usually an optional extra. The cheapest fittings are in white which is a cold, clinical colour, so it is often necessary to

Some modern designs in bathroom furniture from Armitage Shanks Ltd

supply warmth with rich or brightly coloured wall and floor coverings, and a range of gay towels and accessories. More expensive bathroom suites are available in a variety of shapes, sizes, and rich, glamorous colours. When choosing bathroom equipment, make certain that the bath is long enough and wide enough for the biggest member of the family. A bath can be 1500–1800 mm long, and 700–800 mm wide. It can be made from enamel-coated cast iron or pressed steel, fibreglass or acrylic plastic. Modern acrylic baths have smooth, moulded surfaces. Shapes vary from the standard version to corner-shaped baths, deep square tubs and models designed for two people.

A hand basin can be fitted on a pedestal, in a vanitory unit, across a corner or recessed into a wall. Sizes vary, but it is best to get the largest and deepest bowl which will fit into your design plan. A shower does not take up as much floor space as a bath, and uses less hot water. If a bathroom has a separate shower, it can be a complete cabinet unit, or a wall-hung fitting with a floor tray and a curtained surround. There are also shower fittings which can be used inside a bath.

Most modern bathroom suites have a matching bidet as an optional accessory. The bidet can be fitted on a pedestal or be recessed into a wall. A lavatory can have a flushing or a syphonic action. The cistern can be a standard version standing behind and above the lavatory, a slimline version with panels or it can be concealed in the wall.

A comparatively new idea is the fitted bathroom. Neat and attractive modular units are used to house the bath, hand basin, bidet and lavatory. Some have smooth lids which, when lowered, turn the units into streamlined seating surfaces.

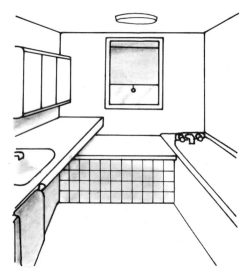

Many bathrooms have one central ceiling light. The light fitting should be made of plastic or glass. Metalled surfaces would gradually be affected by the steamy atmosphere. An enclosed fitting which fits flush to the ceiling or wall is ideal. Fluorescent strip or tube lighting can be used over bathroom cabinets or mirrors, and these can be fitted with shaver sockets. Light switches must have a pull-down cord, or be placed outside the bathroom.

If there is a central heating system then hot water will be available from this. Other water-heating equipment:

a an instantaneous gas water heater which can be fixed to a wall or be hidden inside a cupboard (but *only* if it has a balanced flue);

b an instantaneous electric water heater;

c an immersion heater.

A cold bathroom can be heated by means of:

a a heated towel rail (connected to the domestic hot water supply or central heating system);

b an electrically heated towel rail;

c a portable oil-filled radiator (*never* use a portable electric fire in the bathroom);

d a wall-fixed radiant electric heater (with a pull-cord switch);

e a ceiling-fixed radiant electric heater and light combined;

f a wall-fixed infra-red heater;

g a ceiling or wall light and fan heater combined.

All bathroom surfaces should be water and splashproof, and easy to clean.

DIMPLEX HEATING LTD

The bedroom

A functional bedroom is used for **sleeping**, **dressing** and the **storage of clothes**. If the room is large, has good natural lighting, adequate ventilation and an efficient source of heat, it does not make sense to leave it unused for most of the day. Nowadays, many families turn their bedrooms into multi-functional areas which can be used for **hobbies** and **leisure activities** such as reading, listening to records and dressmaking. Teenagers can make their bedrooms into **studys/dens**, and younger children may use bedrooms as **play areas**. All these activities require storage units, as well as a comfortable bed which may be needed for seating space during the day. The traditional bedroom suite consisting of free-standing bed, wardrobe, chest of drawers and dressing table, has therefore given way to sleek, modular units which can be used for a variety of purposes.

In a well-planned multi-purpose bedroom, the storage equipment for each type of activity should be grouped

together to form compact work zones. Recessed alcoves or walls can be fitted with a useful collection of shelves, cupboards, drawers and work surfaces, which are grouped together to save space, time and energy.

A study work zone

A teenager's den

A dressmaking work zone

SCHREIBER FURNITURE LTD

The bed usually takes up the most floor space in a bedroom. Twin beds or a single bed can be placed lengthways along a wall, but a double bed has to jut out into the middle of the room so that there is space on either side. This makes it easier for both people to climb in and out of bed, and also helps when making and changing the bed. A bed should not be placed directly under a window unless the window has been double-glazed. It would be uncomfortable and unhealthy to sleep in draughts from an ill-fitting window. Similarly, it is not advisable to have the bed head next to or in front of a central heating radiator. The bed should be positioned so that it does not block the path between the door and the rest of the furniture. In Figure A it is necessary to walk right round (or clamber over) the bed to reach the storage units. This wastes time and energy. A more sensible arrangement is shown in Figure B.

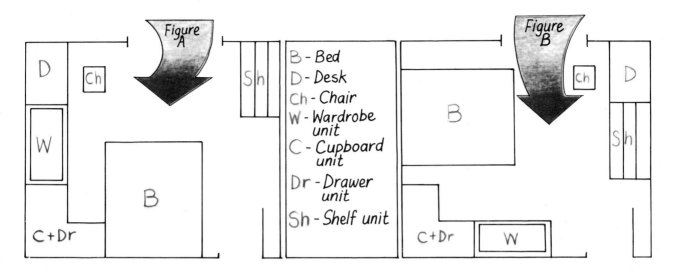

Figure A

Figure B

B - Bed
D - Desk
Ch - Chair
W - Wardrobe unit
C - Cupboard unit
Dr - Drawer unit
Sh - Shelf unit

It is not a good idea to have a dressing table or any other item of furniture blocking the natural light from a window. An efficient arrangement of bedroom furniture has the various items pushed back against the walls or fitted into recesses, allowing the maximum amount of light and sunshine into a room. Where the floor space is limited, it helps to use wall storage units, which reach right up to the ceiling, or beds which have drawers fitted into the base.

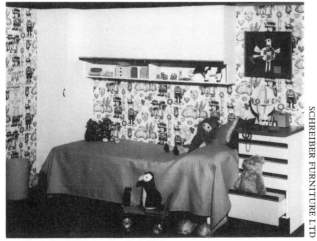

Wall storage units in a child's bedroom

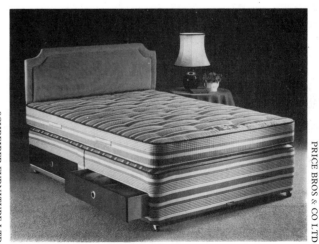

A bed with fitted drawers

Many bedrooms have only one light which is positioned in the centre of the ceiling. This gives insufficient light for any close work. Extra lights should be provided at key points in the room, such as at the dressing table, the study/activity area and above the bed. The dressing table can be lit by pendant lights from the ceiling, angled spotlights on the wall or at the side of the mirror, or strip lighting concealed underneath a wall cupboard. It is better to attach bedside lights to the bedhead or fix them to the wall, rather than have loose table lamps which can be knocked over. If a bedside light is being groped for in the dark, a pull-cord switch is easier to find than a tiny button. A study desk should have good natural and artificial lighting. If the writing surface is placed at right angles to the window, then the writer will not be working in his own shadow. Extra artificial lighting above the desk can be provided by a pendant ceiling light, or angled spotlights. Two-way switches are useful in the bedroom, so that the main ceiling light can be turned off and on at the door and by the bed. If portable lamps are needed at different positions in the room, there should be sufficient power points. Power points in a child's room should have shutters so that they are "poke-proof" and can only be used with the correct plug.

Even though a bedroom may be used for many different day-time activities, it should still be a peaceful, comfortable room in which to relax and sleep. If noises are distracting, try to soundproof the room by:

- **a** sealing air gaps around windows and doors with draught-excluding strips;
- **b** using heavy full-length curtains and fitted carpets;
- **c** fixing cork tiles to wall surfaces;
- **d** installing double-glazed windows with a large insulation gap.

The living/dining room

A comfortable and practical living/dining room does not just happen. It has to be planned in detail. Using graph paper and a scale of 1 mm to 25 mm, draw an outline of a living/dining room. On the plan indicate the position of doors, windows, fireplace, radiators etc. Here is an example.

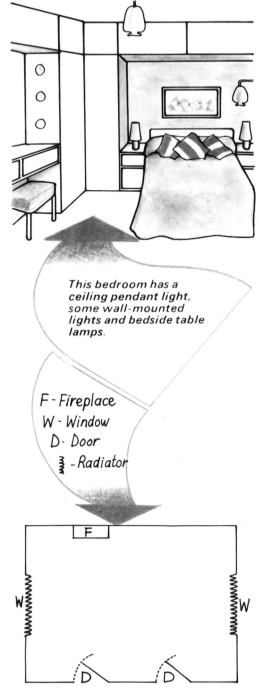

This bedroom has a ceiling pendant light, some wall-mounted lights and bedside table lamps.

F - Fireplace
W - Window
D - Door
≈ - Radiator

Now list all the activities you associate with this area, e.g.

    relaxing
    conversing
    reading
    entertaining
    eating meals
    watching television
    listening to records
    studying
    writing letters
    sewing
    playing the piano
    playing games or
    enjoying a variety of other hobbies

and consider what items of furniture you require to cope with this range of pursuits. Make scaled cut-out shapes of each piece of furniture and decide how they can be grouped together to make sensible work zones. Try the furniture in different positions on the plan until you find a suitable arrangement.

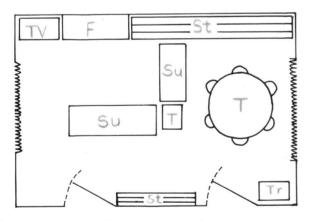
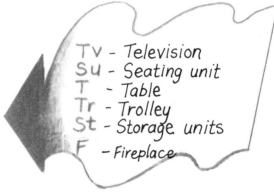

Here are some points to remember.

1 Include plenty of storage units and put them near each activity zone.

2 Allow plenty of space to move between zones.

3 Do not arrange heavy furniture so that it masks power points, blocks light from the windows or lamps, or heat from the radiators.

4 Doors must be able to sweep open completely without causing problems.

5 Make good use of alcoves, recesses and bay windows by slotting furniture into them. The scaled plan will indicate if items of furniture will fit into required positions.

6 Use space sensibly. A small room will be short of floor space, so push the furniture back against the walls. A large room, though, gives more scope. Seats can be arranged:

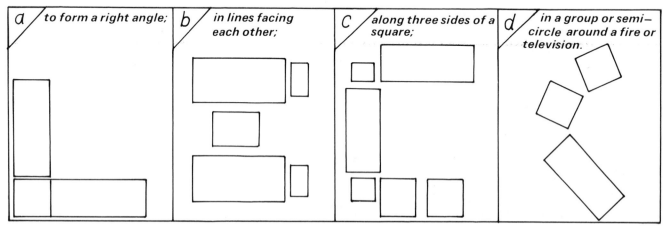

a to form a right angle; *b* in lines facing each other; *c* along three sides of a square; *d* in a group or semi—circle around a fire or television.

7 Furniture for family meals will need to be put near the kitchen or dining hatch to avoid carrying food and dishes a long way. In many modern houses the dining room is an extension of the kitchen, and is only screened from it by a worktop and storage unit. This arrangement provides a convenient eating zone, but noise, steam and smells from the kitchen can be distracting.

A completely separate dining room is useful for special occasion meals, but there should be a connecting door or hatch between the dining room and the kitchen. If one long room has to serve as a dual-purpose lounge/dining area, try to isolate the lounge furniture from the dining furniture. This can be done by using a room divider. A divider is useful for displaying or storing equipment but it should not be allowed to form too solid a barrier because this will affect the feeling of light and space in a room. A fitted storage unit

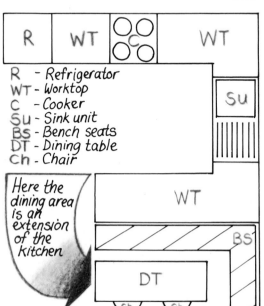

R - Refrigerator
WT - Worktop
C - Cooker
Su - Sink unit
BS - Bench seats
DT - Dining table
Ch - Chair

Here the dining area is an extension of the kitchen

or small table behind the settee will form a useful ledge when serving and eating snack meals, especially if it is the same height as the settee back.

A complete wall of matching storage units can be used to link the two separate zones in a dual-purpose room. This is a useful and practical way of creating more space.

SCHREIBER FURNITURE LTD

8 Arrange the television so that it can be seen from each of the seating areas. It is possible to buy pivoting wall brackets for television sets. The unit can be pushed back against the wall when not in use. Sound and audio-equipment can be positioned on adjustable wall shelves. These take up less space than floor housing units.

9 Try to arrange power points where they will be needed. You may decide to have the following electrical equipment: television set, hi-fi, table and/or floor standard lamps, electric fire or fan heater.

10 A living room should have plenty of artificial light. Subdued background lighting will be needed to prevent eyestrain when watching television, and to give a cosy relaxing atmosphere. Bright concentrated lighting will be required for reading, sewing and studying. The lighting can be:

> *a* overhead (from pendant fittings, or spotlights mounted on tracks);

b fitted to the wall (these can match central fittings to give a co-ordinated look, or be fixed to tracks);

c flexible (e.g. table/floor standard lamps or clip-on spotlights).

Spotlights can be used to highlight a picture, an arrangement of ornaments or a display of indoor plants, and can be adjusted to give a bright light without a harsh glare.

A dining table needs good lighting. This can be from a central rise-and-fall ceiling pendant, or from wall or floor lamps.

This living area has a mixture of overhead, wall and flexible lighting.

BITO (UK) LTD

One-room living

There are many people who, by choice or necessity, experience one-room living. Some bed-sitters or one-room apartments have separate, communal bathrooms and kitchens, but often even these facilities have to be included in the single room. This means that one room has to be equipped for eating, sleeping, washing, relaxing, working and entertaining purposes.

Open-plan living has its advantages. Because there is only one room, it:

a is economical to heat;

b is easy to clean;

c requires a minimum of furniture.

Choose furniture and fittings with care so that you make the best use of the limited space available. It is important to consider your own lifestyle. For example:

1 Will you be living **and** working in the room or just returning to it each evening?

2 Will you need to cook substantial meals or only prepare the occasional snack?

3 Will you need proper laundry equipment, e.g. a washing machine and/or tumble drier or can you use a convenient launderette?

When you have decided on the range of furniture you are likely to need, look around for multi-purpose items which will be functional and not just decorative. It is likely that a seating unit will have to be used for sleeping at night, so select a model which converts into a bed. Look for the kind which can be left "ready-made", as you will find it tiresome to have to re-make a bed each evening. To simplify bed-making use a duvet and fold, close or cover the bed with the fitted bottom sheet still in place. During the day, store the duvet in a drawer, and use the pillows as cushions. If you decide to buy a divan bed, choose one with a firm edge and turn the mattress frequently to even the wear and tear. Use a hard-wearing throwover bedspread or fitted cover during the day. If a divan is pushed back against a wall to save space, it will be too deep to make a comfortable seating unit, so line the wall with thick wedge-shaped cushions or backrests. A pile of gay scatter cushions will help to disguise the fact that it is really a bed.

A sensible alternative arrangement is to construct a raised sleeping platform or loft, which is reached by a ladder. The floor space is then free for all the daytime activities. This is only suitable for rooms with a high ceiling because building regulations state that living spaces must have a ceiling height of at least 2285 mm. Another space-saving idea is to put a mattress on top of an arrangement of fixed storage units, or to build a raised seating platform with a pull-out bed hidden underneath.

A raised sleeping platform reached by a ladder

Simple floor beds can be made from large blocks of foam rubber, or giant "sag-bags". If floor beds are being used continually, it is wise to insulate the room against draughts by edging windows and doors with strips of foam, and using long curtains. Polystyrene sheets or tiles can be used on walls and ceilings.

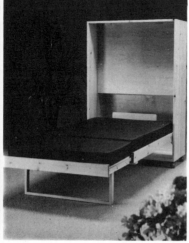

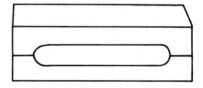

Two space-saving ideas by Relyon

There must be plenty of storage space in a one-room home. This should be fitted to the walls, wherever possible, because built-in units take up less floor space than free-standing ones. A combination of open shelves, chests, cupboards and drawers is ideal. If you want to use dividers to separate the various zones, choose low ones which do not reduce the feeling of light and space. A good idea is to construct a sturdy peninsula unit as a divider and use the inside for storage and the top surface as an eating/working surface. Remember that many divan beds have sliding drawers or mattresses which lift up to give extra storage space.

A bed with sliding drawers

There are various ways of using the ceiling for high-level storage. These range from sturdily constructed platforms, to simple hammocks suspended from wall fittings.

Work surfaces will be needed to:

a eat at;
b work at;
c cook or prepare food on.

A gate-leg table is a useful item of furniture because it can be opened out when in use, and folded away afterwards. It is possible to buy wall cupboards which have let-down leaves to make a working surface. Folding card tables, nests of occasional tables and fitted trolleys can all be used to give extra work space, where necessary.

If extra seating is required, there is a range of modular designs which will fit most shapes of room. They can be fitted into alcoves, recesses and bay windows, and may have storage space underneath the seat cushions. Garden chairs are inexpensive, comfortable and collapsible and, when folded, they can be stored in a very small space. Stackable stools and chairs are also useful.

Cooking equipment and appliances should be grouped together. The smallest one-room flat will need at least an electric kettle and a single hob burner. Other space-saving cooking appliances are:

a a pressure cooker;
b a microwave oven;
c an electric slow cooker;
d an oven with one or two burners;

e an electric grill/rotisserie;

f an electric sandwich maker.

The sink may also be required as a hand basin, so choose a fairly deep bowl which is recessed into a laminated plastic worktop. It is possible to buy mini refrigerators, freezers, washing machines and tumble driers, and where space is scarce, look for models which can stand on worktops or be mounted on walls. Arrange the kitchen equipment to form a triangular work zone (see page 49), and invest in plenty of storage units. Baskets which clip on to the underside of shelves and the inside of cupboard doors make extra storage accommodation.

The kitchen area can be screened from the rest of the room by:

a attractive curtains;

b ceiling-hung pull-down blinds;

c a concertina of louvred doors;

d a sliding partition;

e bead curtains;

f a decorative screen.

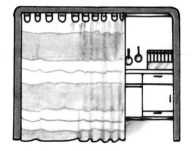

If drying clothes is a problem, take them to a launderette, or invest in:

a a tumble drier;

b an electrically heated drying cabinet (this may have a fan mechanism to blow the clothes dry);

c a pull-out clothes line which can be fixed between two walls;

d a clothes-drying frame which can be folded and put away when not in use;

e a special zip-up polythene bag with a blow-dry heater.

If portable heating equipment is needed, use plug-in radiators, electric fires, fan or convector heaters. There are plug-in oil-fired radiators and portable oil stoves. Night storage heaters are economical because they use off-peak electricity. If there is a constant supply of wood, it may be a good idea to consider a wood-burning stove. Some models heat water and can also be used for cooking food.

Adequate ventilation is important. This can consist of:

a an opening louvred window;

    b an extractor fan in a wall or window;
    c a ducted cooker hood.
  Spotlights can be angled and swivelled to give good artificial lighting for different areas. Rise-and-fall ceiling pendants are useful over tables and worktops. Table and standard lamps are flexible and can be moved around the room as required.

Think and Do

1. In your notebook say how you would:
a. eliminate draughts in a bed-sitter;
b. reduce glare in a kitchen;
c. soundproof a study/bedroom;
d. heat a bathroom.
2. Design a poster to make people aware of the dangers of using portable electrical equipment in the bathroom.
3. What points should be remembered when planning an efficient kitchen layout? Give some advice on:
a. choosing storage units;
b. positioning power points;
c. ventilating a kitchen.
4. Suggest some ways of providing extra storage space in a:
a. kitchen;
b. bedroom;
c. bathroom;
d. lounge/dining area.
5. List some of the advantages and disadvantages of:
a. fluorescent strip lighting;
b. room dividers;
c. convertible beds;
d. bathroom showers.
6. Describe what is meant by the following:
a. flexible lighting;
b. peninsula units;
c. "sag-bags";
d. work zones.

7. What points would you look for when choosing seating and sleeping units for a one-room flat?

8. Write a paragraph about each of the following:

a. artificial lighting in a kitchen;

b. water-heating equipment in a bathroom;

c. multi-purpose furniture in a bedroom;

d. laundry equipment in a bed-sitter.

9. Copy this plan of a living/dining area into your notebook. Imagine you are furnishing the room. List the items you would buy, and on the plan show how you would arrange them.

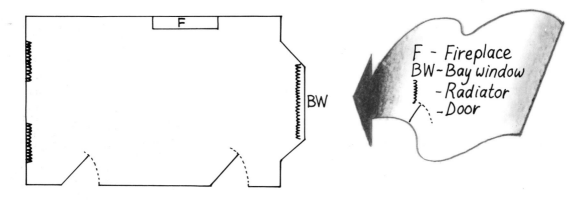

10. What is meant by a dual-purpose room? Suggest some ways of:

a. converting a bedroom into a study/bedroom;

b. making a safe play area for toddlers inside the house;

c. using the extra space in a large hall;

d. providing an eating zone in a kitchen.

CHAPTER 4

The design of furniture and fittings

Furniture design is influenced by the needs of the people, and the materials and manufacturing techniques available at the time. Throughout history, furniture has mirrored the spirit of the age. The eighteenth century produced delicate, elegant furniture of beautiful proportions, which suited the well-to-do people and blended in with the architecture of the period.

Life in the twentieth century is all hustle and bustle, and the design of furniture has echoed the need for speed and efficiency. Lines have become simple and practical. Polished carvings and ornate decorative trims have disappeared in favour of streamlined features which are easy to keep clean. Modern furniture consists of gentle curves and straight lines which give symmetry, balance, and pleasing shapes and proportions. Here is an example of a modern chair. Its strength and comfort depend on simple lines.

Furniture today is colourful and practical, and made from a variety of materials ranging from traditional wood to glass reinforced plastics.

ERCOL FURNITURE LTD

Materials used in the design of modern furniture

Wood has a warm and comfortable feel which has made it popular through the ages. Today, hard woods, such as oak, elm, sycamore, beech, teak and mahogany are used to make solid, hard-wearing items of furniture. They are also made into thin veneers which are bonded to blockboard and other cheap wood substitutes, to produce less expensive furniture. Veneered wood looks attractive but it is not as durable as solid hard wood. Soft woods, such as pine and spruce, mark easily so they are used for the base of veneered furniture or are made into whitewood furniture which is sold unpainted. Chipboard is made by treating wood with resins. It can be covered with a veneer of hard wood or a plastic surface such as Formica or Melamine.

Metals, such as steel, aluminium and light alloys, are used to give strength to furniture without making it bulky or heavy. Modern furniture is, therefore, light in weight, easy to move about and is often characterized by rectangular shapes and straight lines. Metals are also used for the arms and legs of tables and chairs, and for furniture handles.

HABITAT DESIGNS LTD

Fibreglass or glass reinforced plastics can be moulded into simple, elegant shapes which are strong and hard wearing. They are used in the construction of tables and chairs, and help to give modern furniture its lightness, durability and sculptured look.

DESIGN COUNCIL

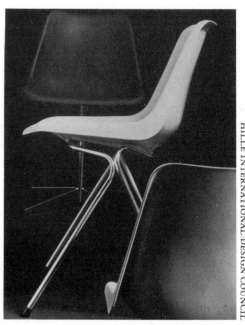

HILLE INTERNATIONAL DESIGN COUNCIL

Wood "finishes"

Wooden furniture is usually made from a solid hard wood, or a hard wood veneer on a soft wood base. Here are some of the finishing surfaces which can be applied to the wood.

*1 **French polish*** This gives a high gloss finish to furniture but it shows marks easily and can be damaged by heat, scratches, solvents and damp. It is usually reserved for old, expensive pieces of furniture which must be handled with care.

*2 **Wax*** This is used on oak and pine furniture. It forms a soft film which picks up dirt and dust easily. Wax can be used as a top coating for furniture which has been coated with polyurethane.

*3 **Polyurethane*** This can be a clear varnish, or a mixture of varnish and stain which colours and decorates in one process. It gives a hard-wearing surface to wood and is not damaged by heat, water, abrasives or solvents. It can have a gloss, satin or matt finish.

*4 **Paint*** This can be an oil-based alkyd resin paint or one of the water-based acrylics which have additives such as vinyl, silthane and polyurethane. It forms a hard-wearing gloss, satin or matt surface which is easy to clean. Paint is usually used for kitchen and nursery furniture.

*5 **Cellulose*** This produces a very hard-wearing surface which is not easily marked. It can be used for tables and chairs.

Living room furniture

A living room should be designed for relaxation. The furniture should be carefully chosen to be attractive, comfortable and suitable to the needs of the people using it. A family with young children will need items of furniture which are hard wearing, whereas careful adults may wish to surround themselves with expensive antiques which they can lovingly cherish. Colour, pattern and texture should always be used carefully to add interest and appeal.

Modern living room furniture is versatile and practical. Wall storage units, which consist of an arrangement of cupboards, shelves and drawers, are popular. They can house a variety of items such as the television set, books, ornaments, table lamp, drinks unit, hi-fi set, potted plants, photographs and games. By arranging the units against the walls, a large amount of storage space is created without the room looking cramped and cluttered. Most storage units are designed to a modular system, which means that they can be added to when necessary, and shelves and cupboards can be re-arranged or interchanged to suit a family's requirements. Storage units can be free-standing or they can be fixed to the walls on batons. Free-standing units are more expensive but they can be moved about the room and are not permanent fixtures. It is a good idea to build storage units into existing alcoves and recesses. This makes a room seem larger.

When choosing storage units make certain there is enough space for all the items you want to store. Open shelves look attractive when a few special objects are on display, but they look untidy if they are overcrowded, so check that there are sufficient covered areas in which to "hide" the ordinary items of everyday life. Remember that open shelves collect dust, and a busy household may prefer to have glass-fronted cabinets to cut down on the cleaning required. Shelves should be adjustable so that they can be moved to different positions, and drawers and cabinet doors should open and close easily. Flap doors which open upwards or downwards need firm hinges and there should be sufficient space to open them completely. A drop-flap door makes a useful serving or writing surface. Drawer and door handles can be made of metal or wood. Sometimes they are carved out of the front of the drawer or door, or "finger-holds" are shaped from the solid wood. It is possible to plan and assemble a complete floor-to-ceiling storage wall, but check that the units either fit flush to the floor, or are raised so that it is easy to clean underneath. Before buying, look at the back of wall units. See that:

B & I NATHAN LTD

  a all surfaces have been well finished;
  b joints have been made correctly and right-angled pieces have not just been glued together;
  c good-quality wood has been used for the backs of cabinets and the bottoms of drawers.

Seats in a living room should look attractive and comfortable. Many people still choose the traditional three-piece suite, but the size of modern rooms often suggests a different approach. Small rooms can look overcrowded with a large three-seater settee and two separate armchairs, and one of the following ideas might be more suitable.

1 Modular seating units where seats and table surfaces can be interchanged. This gives a flexible seating arrangement which can be pushed back against the walls, be grouped at right angles or in various positions.

2 Two two-seater settees with a matching fireside chair.

3 A two-seater settee with separate chairs.

4 Armless individual seats which can be pushed together or used separately.

5 One large settee and a series of huge floor cushions.

Whichever seating arrangement is preferred, always try to make the best use of the floor space available. Remember that if large items of furniture are placed in the middle of the floor, the room will look smaller. Where possible arrange seats against a wall or in an alcove or recess. A friendly arrangement is to group seats in a right angle with a carpet square or attractive rug to define the seating area. This idea can be used to separate the seating and eating zones in a combined living/dining room.

E GOMME LTD

A two-seater and a three-seater settee and an individual armchair allow flexible seating arrangements

In this room the furniture has been arranged against the walls and in recesses.

Chair frames can be made from:

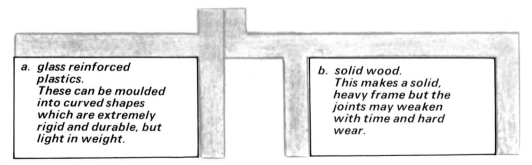

a. *glass reinforced plastics. These can be moulded into curved shapes which are extremely rigid and durable, but light in weight.*

b. *solid wood. This makes a solid, heavy frame but the joints may weaken with time and hard wear.*

Two upholstery materials used widely nowadays are latex foam and polyurethane foam. They are light in weight and extremely comfortable. Chair covers can be made from a wide variety of fabrics, such as wool, leather, imitation leather or PVC, dralon, tweed, linen, cotton, nylon, corduroy, crushed velvet and wool/synthetic mixtures. When choosing upholstery fabrics look for durability, ease of cleaning and colours which will not fade quickly. Some fabrics are treated with a stain- or dirt-resistant finish, and it is always worth checking to see if seat covers can be zipped off for dry cleaning. Here are some points to remember when choosing seating arrangements for a living room.

1 A high-backed chair gives support to the head and shoulders, but some people prefer the freedom of a low back. It is often possible to buy matching high- and low-backed chairs.

2 The seat base should be long enough to give support to the upper parts of the legs, and high enough to allow both feet to rest comfortably on the floor without causing pressure at the back of the knees.

3 Heavy chairs and settees should be fitted with glides or castors.

4 If seat arms are required, they should be at the correct height. Upholstered arms are comfortable but wooden ones are firmer to grasp when getting up out of a chair. Deep wings eliminate draughts but they can get in the way when holding a conversation with somebody next to you.

5 A chair should feel comfortable, so always sit in it before buying.

6 Look for signs of good workmanship, e.g. patterns which match across settee cushions, and neat under-surfaces to seats.

7 Some settees and chairs convert to form beds. This type is worth considering if there is a shortage of money or space, or if an extra bed is required for the overnight guest.

Many modern seating arrangements are grouped around a useful coffee table. A coffee table needs to be at the correct height so that it is convenient for a seated person to use. The table can be made of wood, glass or metal, but it is sensible to choose a stain- and heat-resistant material for the top surface. Slate, marble, glass, ceramic tiles or plastic laminates are suitable. A nest or stack of tables can be a useful addition to a living room and can be stored against a wall when not in use. Avoid choosing a coffee table which has sharp corners. They will result in bruised shins and will be particularly hazardous to young children.

B & I NATHAN LTD

B & I NATHAN LTD

Dining room furniture

When choosing dining room furniture it is important to consider the type of wear it is likely to receive. If there are young children in the family, the dining room may have to be used for homework or as a play area, and it will be necessary to choose sturdy, hard-wearing furniture which will be scratch-resistant and easy to clean. Where the dining room is not required for a dual purpose, this need not be a problem.

Usually dining furniture is kept to a minimum, and all that is required is a table with seats, and a storage unit to hold all the eating equipment, e.g. cutlery, crockery, glasses, place mats and table linen. A dining table can be made from solid wood but it is more likely to be a good quality veneer on cheap wood. Remember that waxed and French polished surfaces are harder to look after than heat- and stain-resistant finishes, such as cellulose or polyurethane lacquer and plastic laminates (see wood "finishes", page 71).

There are several different shapes and designs of tables. A rectangular-shaped table is best for a small room. It can always be pushed against a wall or into a corner or recess if necessary. A circular table takes up more space, but helps to create a friendly atmosphere, and accommodates several people. An extending table is always a good idea because it can be adjusted to the number of people being entertained.

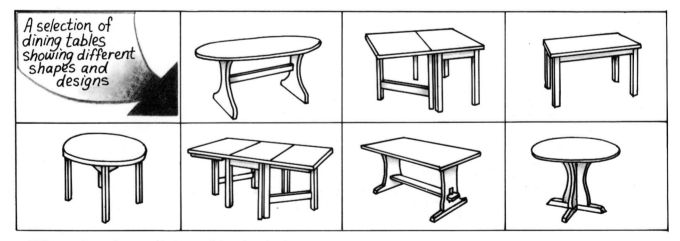
A selection of dining tables showing different shapes and designs

When choosing a dining table check that you can sit at it comfortably and that your knees do not catch against the legs or frame. Make certain that it is large enough for the family, and firm and steady when leaned upon. Look underneath the table to see if it has been finished off well, and check that extension leaves are supported firmly when in position.

Dining chairs should be sturdy and well balanced. They should be the right height to allow an adult to sit with his knees under the table. The backs of the chairs should feel comfortable, and the bases should be wide enough to support the body. Look for simple, sleek lines, and avoid chairs which have awkward dust traps or decorative carvings which will be difficult to clean. Seats can be upholstered with loose or fixed cushions, or be left hard, whichever is preferred, but it is worth choosing a washable surface if there are young children in the family. Some dining chairs have removable covers which are easily washed, and many modern upholstery fabrics can be wiped clean.

E GOMME LTD

If a long refectory-type table is chosen, sturdy bench seats which can be pushed under the table are ideal. Individual chairs or stools can be used at the ends of the table. Where a dining table is placed in the corner of a room or in an alcove it is worth considering a right-angled arrangement of fitted bench seats. This leaves two sides of the table free, a space-saving idea which makes serving a meal much easier.

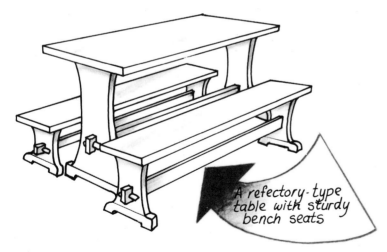

A refectory-type table with sturdy bench seats

The traditional fitted sideboard is still popular. Today's designs are either long and low, or tall like a Welsh dresser. Some people prefer to use fitted wall units and if the room is a combined living/dining area one joint wall fitment can link both zones. If the dining area is very close to the kitchen, and there is a convenient serving hatch, a trolley

B & I NATHAN LTD

B & I NATHAN LTD

Wall storage units are useful in the living room

may be all that is needed to transfer the eating equipment from the kitchen cupboards to the table.

When choosing a sideboard, check that it is big enough to hold all the necessary items. There should be ample cupboard and shelf storage, and a sectioned drawer or loose tray for cutlery. The sideboard should have one surface at a comfortable height so that it can be used for serving food. Shelves should feel sturdy and strong and capable of taking the weight of a full dinner service. Check that drawers and doors open easily and have handles which are comfortable to hold.

Kitchen furniture

The kitchen is the working heart of the home, so it should be an attractive room which is carefully planned. An efficient kitchen starts with the layout or correct positioning of equipment, but the choice of well-designed furniture helps to create the overall effect. Whether a kitchen is large or small, unusually shaped or symmetrical, it should contain ample storage space and at least one continuous flat working surface. Storage units should be built to fit the shape of the kitchen, so that efficient use is made of the whole area.

There are a variety of designs, but most consist of base units with counter tops. These ground level cabinets contain drawers and cupboards with shelves. Some cupboards are fitted with accessories, such as bins and racks which pivot out when the door is opened. Matching wall cupboards can extend right to the ceiling, and open or glass-fronted shallow shelves at shoulder height are convenient for storing spices and flavourings.

When choosing kitchen units look for hard-wearing surfaces which are easy to keep clean. Plastic laminates are ideal. Natural wood has become popular for kitchen storage units but this type should have an easy-clean working surface of plastic laminate, ceramic tiles or marble, and the wood should be treated with a stain-resistant cellulose or polyurethane lacquer. A new feature is the curved counter top which has a rolled front edge and a curved upstand at the wall. These shaped counter tops are easy to keep clean because there are no cracks and crevices, and sharp corner edges are eliminated.

A well-designed kitchen unit should have a recess at floor level so that it is possible to stand comfortably at the working surface with one's toes tucked under the recess. Doors should have adjustable hinges so that they can be lifted off for cleaning, and flat or recessed handles which do not protrude. Catches and handles should work efficiently, and it is helpful to have alternative positions for shelves.

When choosing kitchen units look at the inside surfaces of drawers and cupboards. Check that they are smooth and have a hard-wearing finish. Slide drawers in and out to see if they move easily. Choose warm, pleasant colours and avoid bright, dynamic patterned surfaces which can irritate the eyes. Units in a two-toned colour scheme are attractive.

The kitchen sink is used for a wide variety of jobs, ranging from washing up, preparing food and laundrywork, to household cleaning tasks, watering the garden and washing the car. It is important, therefore, to have a well-designed and efficient model which looks attractive and is easy to clean.

A sink may have a single or double draining board, usually moulded in one piece with the sink bowl. Some modern kitchen units have an inset sink which can be slotted into a continuous, laminated plastic working surface. This eliminates the joints between draining board and adjacent counter top, but can mean that water drips on to the floor from draining utensils. An inset sink should, therefore, be used with a dishwasher, a second sink or a special worktop with draining grooves moulded in the laminated plastic.

Today's range of sink units is very hard wearing. The most popular material is stainless steel but some sinks can be bought with a vitreous enamel, white porcelain, plastic or ceramic finish. A well-designed sink has a splashback behind the unit and may have a rolled front edge to match the curved counter tops of storage units.

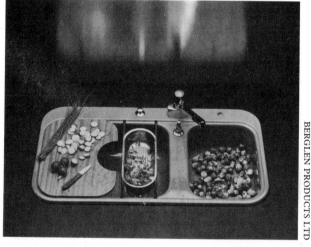

BERGLEN PRODUCTS LTD

BERGLEN PRODUCTS LTD

The sink bowl can be round, square or oblong, and can have shaped accessories such as a draining basket, chopping board and rack for preparing vegetables, which fit over the bowl. Some sinks are equipped with a waste disposal unit which grinds up food waste and debris, and passes it directly to the drains, or there may be an additional centre bowl for waste collection. The cupboard under the sink top can be valuable storage space and may contain a deep drawer for cutlery, and a wire basket attached to the door for storing cleaning products. Some units have an automatic opening wastebin underneath or a fitted dishwasher.

Modern kitchen unit accessories from Moben Continental Kitchens Ltd

Backache can be caused by bending over a sink which is too low, so it is worth experimenting to find the correct height. A sink unit is usually positioned against an outside wall, but in large kitchens it can be plumbed into an island unit like the one illustrated on page 49 to make it accessible from all sides.

Bedroom furniture

The small size of modern bedrooms has meant that designers have had to provide a completely new range of furnishings to use the limited space as efficiently as possible. The ornate, old-fashioned bedroom suite, with its heavy, free-standing wardrobe, dressing table, chest of drawers and tall bedstead, has disappeared in favour of lightweight practical furniture which is characterized by sleek lines and smooth surfaces.

A bedroom today is used for a variety of activities, and the furniture has to be adaptable and versatile. As well as providing sleeping and storage space, the bedroom may be used as a study area, a playroom, a sewing area, a place for watching television or relaxing with a book. The need for multi-purpose furniture has resulted in low divan beds, often without a headboard, which are suitable for sitting and lounging on. Simple tables, shelves, drawers and cupboards have replaced the free-standing wardrobe and dressing table, and the new style of furniture has been pushed back against the walls to create more floor space. Some designs can be built in to alcoves or recesses, or actually attached to the wall surfaces on battens. These create more space in a bedroom and make cleaning easier, though they have the disadvantage of being permanent fittings which cannot be moved into different positions, or be transferred if you move to another house.

There are many modular designs of bedroom furniture which can be bought as single units and built up to provide a complete wall of storage fittings reaching right up to the ceiling. Most designs include fitted wardrobes, shelves, drawers, corner units and dressing table tops, which may have such extras as concealed lighting and lift-up lids with mirror and a cosmetic shelf. Some also include a matching table, linen box, drop-fronted writing bureau, and an assortment of storage cabinets. Free-standing bedroom units should have flat sides so that individual pieces fit flush together. This allows them to be assembled in different positions to suit the shape and size of the bedroom. Low units should be arranged to give a flat, continuous surface, which is easy to clean and useful for displaying ornaments.

Materials are lightweight but durable. Wood veneers, plastic-laminated chipboard and polyurethane-lacquered chipboard are popular. Colours range from polar white to oak and teak. Whitewood bedroom furniture can be finished in any colour of hard-wearing paint.

Here are some points to look for when choosing bedroom storage units.

1 Make certain that there is hanging space for long and short items of clothing. A horizontally placed hanging rail means that clothes can be seen and removed easily, but check that the interior depth of the wardrobe unit is at least 50 cm, so that clothes can hang freely without being crushed.

2 A bedroom should contain plenty of drawer and shelf space. Check that there is room for shoes and bulky items such as hats, thick sweaters and suitcases.

3 When choosing storage units buy the best you can afford. Look for signs of quality and good workmanship: strong door hinges; smooth-running drawers; tightly fitting joints; continuous pattern matching of veneers; solid side, bottom

and back panels; matching waxed surfaces on inside and out; smooth inside surfaces which will not snag clothes; efficient latches and locks; no traces of glue; even spacing around sides, top and bottom of drawers; and recessed back panels to give added strength.

A nursery or bedroom for a young child should have plenty of storage units. Old trunks, gaily-painted tea chests and stackable plastic bowls are ideal for toys, books and games, and adjustable open shelves are useful for storing baby equipment. Special furniture units can be bought which combine a child's wardrobe with a set of drawers and matching cupboards. When choosing nursery furniture look for hard-wearing surfaces which are smooth and easy to keep clean. Door handles should be chunky and easy to grasp, and drawers should open and close smoothly. Avoid units which have sharp features which could injure a child, and check that all painted surfaces are lead-free.

A modern bed consists of a mattress on top of a firm- or soft-edged base. If a bed is to be used for sitting on as well as for sleeping, a firm-edged base will be better. A soft-edged base has a luxurious feel but does not wear as well. The mattress should be comfortable but firm enough to support the body evenly. It can be made of:

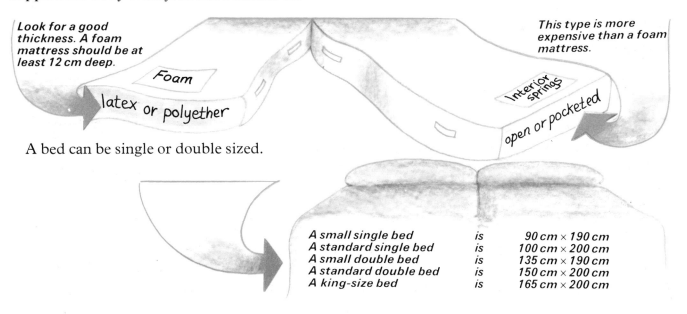

Look for a good thickness. A foam mattress should be at least 12 cm deep.

Foam

latex or polyether

This type is more expensive than a foam mattress.

Interior springs

open or pocketed

A bed can be single or double sized.

A small single bed	is	90 cm × 190 cm
A standard single bed	is	100 cm × 200 cm
A small double bed	is	135 cm × 190 cm
A standard double bed	is	150 cm × 200 cm
A king-size bed	is	165 cm × 200 cm

If space is limited, it can be a good idea to consider:

a bunk beds;

b folding beds;

c stacking beds;

d convertible beds.

Here are some points to look for when choosing a bed.

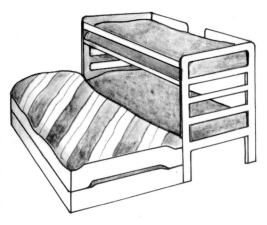

1 Always buy the best you can afford. A cheap bed will be of inferior quality and will not wear well. Choose a reputable make and look for the BSI kitemark.

2 Check that the bed is long enough to support the whole body, and wide enough to allow ease of movement.

3 Choose a firm mattress and avoid ones which seem to sag or dip. Remember that a quilted, decorative finish is flat and easy to clean, but a deeply-buttoned effect can be uncomfortable to lie on and will collect dust.

4 Do not be tempted to choose a mattress by the look of the cover or "ticking". Always ask what material is inside.

5 Choose a mattress and base which are the right height. If a bed is too high or too low, it can be difficult to get in and out of.

When choosing a cot, check that the space between the bars measures 75–100 mm so that a baby cannot trap his head, arms or legs. A cot usually has one drop-side and it is important to check that the fastening mechanism is child-proof, with no sharp edges which could harm the baby. The space between the bottom of the bars and the base of the cot should be narrower than the thickness of the mattress, to prevent the baby slipping through the gap or trapping his head. It is essential to check that a lead-free paint has been used for decorating the cot, and that there are no plastic-coated nursery transfers which could peel off and be swallowed. The mattress should be firm so that the baby will not sink into it and suffocate, and it should have a smooth, waterproof covering which can be easily wiped clean.

A teenager's bedroom is often a "den" which is used for hobbies, homework, reading, listening to records and entertaining friends. It should be designed more as a bedsitter than as a traditional bedroom, with attractive, hard-wearing units which can be used for a variety of purposes. Adjustable shelves teamed with an assortment of storage units will help to create a multi-functional room. A fitted work table or unit with a drop flap will make a useful writing surface. The bed can be folded away during the day to create more floor space, or can be used as sitting space if a firm-edged divan base is chosen.

Wall-fixed lighting will be more versatile than a central pendant light, and should pivot to focus on reading and working areas. An easy noticeboard can be made with cork wall tiles or felt-covered pinboard. It may also be advisable to consider soundproofing the room by installing a double-glazed window, and using textured soundproof tiles on the walls and ceiling.

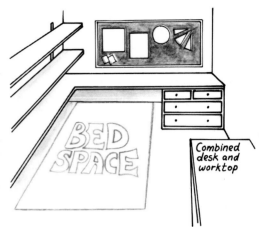

Combined desk and worktop

Bathroom furniture

The bathroom used to be a cold, unattractive and purely functional room but today's man-made materials have revolutionized it. It is now a warm, inviting room in which to relax.

The old-fashioned white porcelain bath, basin and lavatory have been replaced by sophisticated fibreglass and acrylic designs in sleek, streamlined shapes and a wide variety of colours. Some designs have a matching bidet and shower unit. Floors are carpeted for warmth and comfort,

ARMITAGE SHANKS LTD

or are covered in colourful, textured materials such as cushioned vinyl, ceramic tiles, linoleum and marble. There is a wide range of attractive waterproofed wall coverings ranging from paint, wallpaper, vinyl and ceramic tiles, to laminated plastic sheets and sealed wood panelling.

When choosing bathroom furniture and fittings, look for surfaces which are easy to clean. Check that there is sufficient room to wipe around taps and behind the basin and lavatory pedestals. Look for safety features such as bath and shower grab-rails, and non-slip surfaces for baths and floors. See that taps are easy to turn and that basins are at a convenient height. Avoid furniture with sharp edges and choose a bath and basin with curved corners.

Furnishing on a budget

Buying reasonably priced furniture is becoming increasingly difficult, and many young married couples have problems when furnishing their first home. They may choose to:

   a rent furnished accommodation;
   b beg cast-off furniture from relatives and friends;
   c hunt through junk shops, auction rooms and house sales for suitable items;
   d scan newspaper advertisements for second-hand furniture;
   e buy furniture and appliances on HP (hire purchase) or extended credit;
   f buy the minimum of furniture necessary and add extra items when they can afford them;
   g make do-it-yourself furniture.

There are advantages and disadvantages to each of these methods. Discuss them with your friends.

Here are some budget ideas and sensible economies to consider when furnishing a home.

1 When looking at second-hand furniture, try to look beyond the outward appearance. Remember that:

   a unattractive varnishes can be removed;
   b rough wood can be sanded down and sealed or painted;
   c upholstery can be renewed, and worn braiding and fringing can be replaced;

   d cushions can be restuffed;

   e old-fashioned dining chairs can be recovered;

   f loose covers can be made for easy chairs and settees;

   g mirrors can be resilvered.

It may be worth going to woodwork classes or an evening course on renovating furniture. Furnishing a home this way is great fun and there is a rewarding sense of achievement at the end. Before buying second-hand wooden furniture, check that it is basically sound. Inspect it carefully. Look underneath and at the back, and check for signs of quality, such as efficient drawers, locks and hinges, recessed back panels, smooth and waxed internal surfaces, and sturdy joints. If the wood is warped or the joints weak, do not buy. Look for small pin-sized holes and fine sawdust which are tell-tale signs of woodworm. Check that the springs on chairs and settees are sound.

2 If carpeting is too expensive, use scatter rugs on a wooden floor. Old floorboards can be sanded and sealed, or a new wooden floor can be laid quite cheaply by covering the existing floor with thin plywood sheets. Hard-wearing mats such as sisal and hair cord, or a non-woven synthetic fibre carpet make economical floor coverings. Interchangeable carpet tiles and carpet squares are also worth considering. Very cheap, hard-wearing rag rugs can be made by cutting up old clothes and working the strips into a hessian backing.

If you can afford a carpet, choose a good one. It is false economy to buy a cheap one of inferior quality. Save by shopping around for the best prices. Visit carpet warehouses and carpet shops which have genuine sales. Ask to see the stock of off-cuts. These are reasonably priced remnants of carpeting, in various sizes and quality.

3 Economize with window coverings. If you do require curtains, try making your own. Look around market stalls for bargains in fabrics, and prepare your own decorative hanging poles. Curtains can often be made quite economically from dress material, but do choose a good quality, shrink-resistant fabric. You may like to experiment with old, sound sheets and tie and dye a decoration to make an unusual window covering. Paper or wooden slatted blinds are often cheaper than curtains, or a do-it-yourself enthusiast can make roller blinds from the special kits available in the shops.

4 When buying furniture which you want to add to later on, choose well-known module systems which are not likely to be discontinued. Look around furnishing stores for genuine reductions, and then compare the prices at a furniture cash and carry warehouse. Remember to check for "hidden" costs, such as transport and delivery charges. If an item is reduced because it is damaged or substandard, be confident that you can repair it before deciding to buy.

5 A reasonably priced bed can be made by building a base using the instructions from a DIY manual, and then buying a foam mattress to go on top. It is worth remembering that a mattress with a plain ticking may be equally as good as one with a fancy cover, but will probably be cheaper. Giant foam floor cushions can double as sleeping and seating units, and convertible chairs and settees are useful where floor space is limited. For emergency clothes storage in a bedroom, use an old wooden coat-stand, a second-hand dress rack or a clothes line suspended across an alcove or recess. These can be hidden from view by a colourful curtain or attractive screen. Painted or papered wooden boxes make useful storage spaces for toys, books, games, shoes, handbags, etc., and folded clothes can be stored in suitcases.

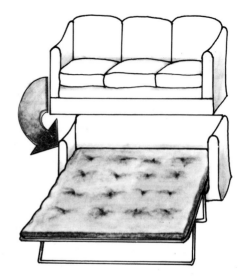

6 In the living room reasonably priced seating units can be bought in the form of floor cushions, colourful "garden" loungers, bench seats with fitted cushions, folding metal or wooden chairs, and firm-edged divans. Wall shelves can be made by laying old floorboards, strips of chipboard or Melamine-covered chipboard across metal uprights and brackets. A basic table/desk can be assembled by placing a flush door across two wooden trestles, or using two small filing cabinets for the supports. This second method has the advantage of providing additional drawer space. Economical light fittings can be made by stripping old shades down to the metal frames and then recovering them with an attractive translucent material.

7 Whitewood cupboards are useful in the kitchen, and wall shelves can be used for saucepans, cooking utensils and crockery. Hooks can be screwed under the bottom shelf for cups etc., and there are several types of sliding wire containers which can be attached to open shelves. When buying household appliances such as heaters, cooker, refrigerator and washing machine, it is a good idea to ask if there are any reconditioned or demonstration models being sold cheaply by the local gas or electricity boards. Electrical discount cash and carry warehouses may stock the appliance you need at a competitive price, so do compare costs.

8 When choosing bathroom furniture, remember that a shower is cheaper to buy than a bath, and uses less hot water.

A fair deal when buying furniture

Nowadays, many items of furniture are made from chipboard or plywood which is covered with a wood veneer. Some cheaper ranges of furniture are made to resemble wood veneer by using a simulated wood finish. This may be just a wood grain paper finish applied to the surface of plain wood. To guard against inferior materials, always ask what furniture is made from. Furniture which is described as:

> **teak** should be solid teak;
>
> **teak veneer** should have a genuine teak veneer;
>
> **teak finish** only "resembles" teak.

If an item of furniture has the "Touch Wood" label, this indicates that it is made from a genuine veneer.

> The Branded Furniture Society
> The British Furniture Manufacturers' Federated Associations
> The National Association of Retail Furnishers
> The National Bedding Federation Ltd
> The Scottish House Furnishers' Association

have joined together to produce a "Furniture Code of Practice" to protect the consumer before buying, when buying and after buying furniture. Shops which display this sign have agreed to follow the Code.

When furnishing a home it is important to choose well-designed heating and lighting fittings. They should be efficient to use, suitable for the different areas and activities involved, and should blend with the other items of furniture.

Heating a home

When choosing a heating system, consider:

    a the cost of the fuel;
    b the availability of the fuel;
    c the efficiency of the heating system;
    d the design of the appliances;
    e whether or not the appliances blend with the design of the room.

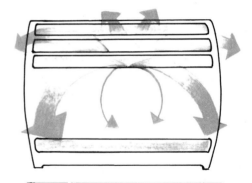

A heating system can warm a room by **radiation** or **convection**. Radiated heat is heat given off in waves or rays, like the sun's heat. It is a cheerful form of heat which has a pleasant effect on the skin. Convected heat is heat which circulates and warms the air in a room.

An open fire feels warm and looks warm. It has a pleasant, radiant heat and helps to create a homely, cheerful atmosphere. An open fire makes an attractive focal point of a room, and it provides natural ventilation which prevents the air from becoming dry and stuffy. An open fire will burn coal, smokeless fuel or wood. If you live in the country it is worth considering wood as a fuel. Logs burn well giving off a crackling heat, and they are cheaper to buy than coal or smokeless fuels. However, an open fire creates dust and dirt, and can give off soot and gases which pollute the atmosphere. An open fire with a back boiler heats the domestic hot water supply and can be used to heat up to seven or eight central heating radiators. A fireplace can be small, unobtrusive and simply designed, or it can have an elegant surround. Wood, stone, marble, brick and slate are traditional materials for fireplaces. Some modern designs have chrome, copper or stainless steel trims, and canopies extending to the ceiling.

In modern, open-plan houses an open fire may not be an efficient means of heating the whole living area, and a built-in or free-standing solid fuel stove may be better. A stove is a good way of heating a large room. It gives off convected and radiant heat when the stove doors are open. A solid fuel stove is made from cast-iron enamel which can be finished in a range of attractive colours. Some have chrome, wood, stainless steel or black stove enamel surfaces.

An open or closed solid fuel fire should always be guarded if there are children under the age of twelve. A sturdy

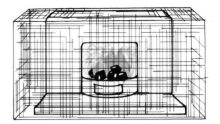

fireguard which can be firmly fixed to a wall, floor or fire-place is safer than a free-standing guard which can be knocked over. An extending fireguard is useful because it will fit different widths of fireplace. Choose a fine-meshed guard which has a top protective ledge. This prevents toys from being pushed through or over on to the fire.

A gas or electric fire involves less effort and is cleaner than a solid fuel fire. It is easy to regulate or control, and gives an almost instant heat. It can be fitted inside an existing fireplace or mounted against a plain wall. A gas fire is efficient and attractive, and has an automatic instant-spark ignition to give a cheerful, visual heat. Most require a chimney. Some have a balanced flue and so have to be fitted to an outside wall. An electric fire may be fixed to a wall or it can be portable, working off any 13 or 15 amp power point. A modern gas or electric fire gives off radiant and/or convected heat. The fire can have the effect of illuminated burning logs, coke or coal. Gas and electric fire cabinets can be made from veneered wood, copper- or bronze-coloured metal, or stainless steel.

An electric fan heater blows hot air around a room. It is an efficient way of heating a cold room but expensive to run for long periods. A night storage heater uses off-peak electricity to give a constant source of heat during the day, so it is an economical means of heating cold, draughty areas such as halls, landings and extensions. Some storage heaters can be regulated to give off different levels of heat, and some have built-in fans to circulate the warm air quickly. A well-designed storage heater is slim and inconspicuous.

A portable oil stove is inexpensive to run and needs little attention, apart from an occasional clean, but the paraffin has to be bought and stored. Filling the heater can be messy. Modern oil stoves are neat and attractive, and most models conform to strict safety regulations but it is important to remember never to move an oil stove when it is lighted or place it where it can be knocked over. It is possible to buy an oil stove which has an automatic lighting device.

Another means of heat is the portable oil-fired electric radiator which can be plugged into a 13 or 15 amp power point. The heat is thermostatically controlled. Always check that the flexes from portable appliances do not trail along the floor, creating safety hazards.

Many home heating systems have no visible source of heat. The rooms are centrally heated by means of:

a slim, inconspicuous radiators (some run along skirting panels so that they do not affect the design of a room);

b ducts of warm air;

c electric elements concealed in the floor or ceiling.

Central heating can be regulated easily and efficiently. It can be automatically controlled to switch on and off as required. Central heating can provide a low level of background heat to be used with an open fire, a gas or electric fire. Full central heating means that no other form of heating is necessary. Well-designed radiators have slim, smooth panels with no dirt-collecting crevices. They can be decorated to match or contrast with the walls behind them. Wall-fixed radiators should be positioned so that they do not obstruct the arrangement of furniture.

Here are some well-designed heating appliances.

A gas fire

An oil-filled radiator

An electric fire

A skirting board convector heater

A convector heater mounted on a wall

Lighting a home

Good artificial lighting is essential in a home. It prevents eyestrain and accidents, and is as important as colour schemes and furnishings in creating the atmosphere of a room.

The type of lighting required depends on the function of a room. Some areas, such as the kitchen, bathroom, hall, stairs and landing, are only used for certain activities, and this makes it easy to choose suitable light fittings and fix them permanently in convenient positions. Other rooms, though, are used for a wide variety of activities, and this means that the lighting must be flexible so that it can be directed towards different areas, as it is required. A collection of low-wattage lights, arranged at different positions in a room, is far more versatile than a single central ceiling pendant.

The source of light is usually a **tungsten filament** ordinary lamp, or a **fluorescent** tube.

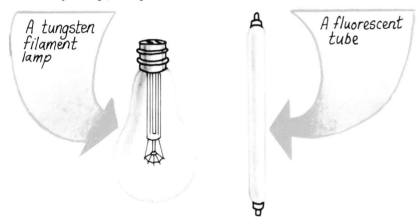

A tungsten filament lamp

A fluorescent tube

Most filament lamps are pear-shaped or mushroom-shaped. Mushroom lamps are neat, compact and easy to handle but they are more expensive than pear-shaped lamps, and they give off more heat, so they should never be used in enclosed or tight fittings. Filament lamps burn for approximately 1000 hours. "Long-life" lamps last for twice as long as filament lamps but they use more electricity, so they are really only worth considering for fittings which are inaccessible. Lamps can be made from clear, pearl, white or

Pear-shaped   Mushroom-shaped

coloured glass. Clear and pearl lamps give off the same amount of light but clear lamps cast dark shadows and pearl lamps cast softer shadows. White lamps give an almost shadowless light. Reflector lamps have a built-in reflecting surface to give a beam of light. Some reflector lamps give wide beams for floodlighting and others give narrow beams for spotlighting.

A reflector lamp

Fluorescent tubes give off more light than filament lamps and last longer. They produce a white light which is shadowless. Some fluorescent tubes give a bright, cold light. Tubes which give a pleasant colour, unfortunately produce less light. De Luxe Warm White filament tubes are probably the best kind for use in the home.

There are many different types of lamp fittings. The main ones are:

a **pendant** fittings which hang from the ceiling;

b fittings which are **surface mounted** on walls and ceilings;

c fittings which are **recessed** into ceilings;

d **spotlights** which can be angled to throw concentrated beams of light;

e **rise-and-fall** pendant fittings;

f **table** fittings for concentrated local lighting;

g **floor standard** fittings for concentrated local lighting.

HABITAT DESIGNS LTD

Lamp fittings distribute light in different ways. Light which is directed downwards is called **direct light**, and light which is directed upwards is called **indirect light**. **Diffusing** fittings give general or even lighting in all directions.

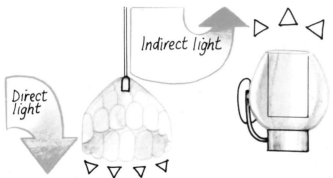

Direct light

Indirect light

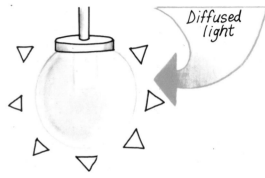

Diffused light

Here are some points to remember when choosing and using lamps and fittings.

1 Never use bare filament lamps without fittings or shades. They will be too bright and glaring. Fluorescent lamps should be fitted with diffusers to conceal the tube.

2 Choose central ceiling fittings for all-round general light, and "spotlight" areas of close work with table or floor fittings, or angled spotlights. When spotlighting, try to avoid glare by angling the lamp away from the eyes.

3 To prevent eyestrain when watching television, have a gentle, subdued light in the room. This will reduce the glare from the set.

4 Rise-and-fall pendant fittings are suitable for background lighting or for lighting dining tables.

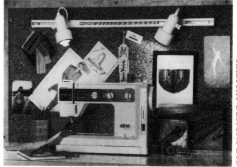

5 Lighting track allows one power point to be used for a number of separate lights. The track can be surface mounted on walls or ceilings, or it can be recessed. Lamps with special adaptors can be plugged anywhere along its length.

6 Electric lamps give off heat. Some fittings or shades will only take up to a certain wattage before they are damaged by the heat, so always check that a fitting will take the wattage of lamp you will be using. The wattage of a lamp is marked on the glass, and the maximum wattage suitable should be marked on the fitting. Spotlights also produce considerable heat, so they should be angled away from delicate fabrics or inflammable materials.

7 Dimmer switches allow you to raise or lower the intensity of lighting in a room. They are useful for toning down bright lamps to create a subdued, restful atmosphere.

Dimmer switch

8 Floor and table lamps should have a large shade to give a wide pool of light. The colours of shades can match or contrast with the general decorative scheme, but before buying a coloured shade, check to see that it looks as effective in daylight as it does in artificial lighting.

9 Try to avoid drastic changes in the level of lighting in any one room. Eyestrain can be caused if the eyes have to continually adjust to different intensities of light.

10 Different colours and surfaces reflect light in different ways. White or light colours reflect more light than dark colours, and glossy surfaces reflect more light than matt ones. Therefore, if a lamp is positioned against a white or glossy wall, the reflected light will give more illumination.

11 Different levels and colours of light can create different atmospheres. Reds are warm, stimulating and active colours. Greens are cool, restful and relaxing. Very bright lights can be exciting, but glaring lights will irritate the eyes.

12 All light fittings should be earthed or they should have double-insulated flexes.

Think and Do

1. Give some advice on choosing each of the following:
a. wall storage units for a dining room; ·
b. easy chairs for a family with young children;
c. a kitchen table for snack meals;
d. a second-hand chest of drawers.

2. List some of the materials used when making modern furniture. What special finishes can be applied to:
a. upholstery fabrics;
b. wood?

3. List some of the advantages and disadvantages of heating a living room with an open fire. Suggest a suitable heating appliance for each of the following:
a. a large and draughty hall;
b. a cold nursery bedroom;
c. the dining area of a modern flat;
d. a caravan.

4. In your own words, explain the difference between:
a. natural and artificial lighting;
b. background and full central heating;
c. waxed and French polished surfaces;
d. foam and interior-sprung mattresses.

5. Here is a picture of a modern chair. Do you think it looks comfortable? In your notebook, explain why you like or dislike the chair.

6. Give some advice to a young married couple on furnishing a home inexpensively.

7. Design a study/bedroom for a teenager. List the furniture and fittings which would be needed and then draw a floor plan to show how they could be arranged.

8. Make a study of *either* a famous eighteenth century furniture designer (e.g. George Hepplewhite, Thomas Sheraton, Thomas Chippendale, Robert Adam) *or* a well-known contemporary furniture designer (e.g. Robin Day, Ernest Race, Lucian Ercolani, Terence Conran, Gordon Russell, Archie Shine).

9. Draw a labelled floor plan for a bathroom in a small modern house. Describe the furniture and fittings. Suggest a suitable:

a. floor covering;

b. wall covering;

c. window covering.

What special features could be added to the bathroom to make it safe for elderly people?

10. Copy the following diagram into your notebook and then write a suitable sentence in each of the boxes.

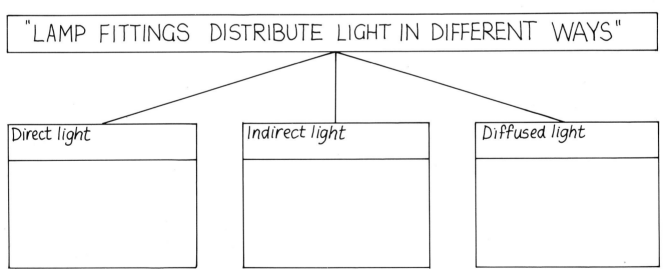

Design suitable light fittings for each of the following:

a. a study area in a bedroom;

b. a dining room furnished with traditional furniture;

c. a staircase with poor natural lighting;

d. a dark kitchen.

The design of household appliances

Cookers

A modern cooker is elegant and streamlined in appearance, efficient to use and may have a bewildering array of special features to help save time and fuel. When choosing a new cooker, it is wise to:

visit any fuel advisory showrooms in your area and collect their advertising leaflets so that you can read all about each model when you get back home. (Important measurements may need to be checked before you make a decision.)

read relevant articles in the Consumers' Association magazine "Which?". (There will be a copy in your library.)

ask friends about the advantages and disadvantages of their particular cooker.

The choice between a gas or electric cooker may depend upon the area in which you live and the availability of the fuel. If gas is not piped to your area, it is pointless to consider buying a gas cooker. Where there is a gas point, the choice between a gas or electric cooker will be influenced by personal preference. Some people like gas because the heat can be instantly controlled and this means that the oven will heat up quicker than an electric one. A gas cooker is not as clean as an electric cooker though, and will not have as many extras as a comparatively priced electric model. Can you think of any more points which will influence your choice?

When you have decided on the type of fuel, you should then think about whether to have a single, free-standing appliance or a separate oven and built-in hob. A free-standing cooker is cheaper to buy but it does create awkward dirt traps. A built-in oven can be positioned at a convenient height to prevent stooping, and this will also put it out of the reach of young children. The separate hob is fitted on a cupboard top or continuous work surface. Some families choose a combination of fuels by having a built-in electric oven with a separate gas hob. This can prove an advantage if there are power cuts. However, a built-in appliance is a permanent fixture and cannot normally be taken away if you move house.

A comparatively new idea is the plug-in, stand-on oven/grill unit which can be placed on any suitable cupboard top and plugged into an ordinary 13 amp socket. This appliance has all the advantages of a built-in oven but can be disconnected easily if you move house or have the kitchen altered. It is important to remember that normal electric cookers require a separate fused socket and must not be plugged into an ordinary 13 amp power point.

It is possible to buy an electric hob with a stainless steel or glass cover which acts as a splashback when the rings are being used and can be folded down to cover the hob when the rings are not in use. This helps to keep the hob unit clean and gives extra work space in the kitchen. There is usually a safety feature which prevents the rings being accidentally turned on after the cover has been lowered.

The modern gas or electric cooker has many special features which help to save time and fuel. Some of these features are available on the cheaper models but usually there are more extras on the dearer priced cookers.

A new development is the built-in gas cooker with matching co-ordinates. The oven and hob are designed to fit closely against kitchen storage units, with the grill and time control panels mounted separately on nearby walls.

Listed overleaf are some of the special features available on a modern gas cooker. Look at the list and discuss which extras you think are essential and which are worth paying more for.

a slow-cooking device which allows the oven to burn at a very low temperature—ideal for keeping food warm or cooking dishes requiring long, slow cooking, e.g. casseroles

simmer stops—a safety device to allow the hot-plate controls to be turned down to a positive simmering position

push-button spark ignition for each burner and for the grill

automatic oven ignition with a re-ignition safety system if the flame goes out

BRITISH GAS

oven flame failure device—safety feature to stop the flow of gas if the burner goes out

a glass-panelled external door or an inner glass door

easy-clean oven linings

a rotisserie for open spit roasting

an autotimer for pre-setting the oven to switch on and off

drop-down wheels for moving the cooker when cleaning

a large-sized oven

an eye-level grill—some models have a fold-away grill

burners which are sealed to the hob and have removable spillage bowls for easy cleaning

a 60-minute minder and a digital time-of-day clock—some models have a radio incorporated in this unit

a surface combustion grill with small flames all over the heating surface to give a larger grilling area

Here are some of the special features available on a modern electric cooker. Look at the list and discuss which extras you think are essential and which are worth paying more for.

a sealed hob with removable spillage trays for easy cleaning, or a lift-up hob with a sealed spillage area beneath

economiser rings

dual circuit rings which allow you to switch on the centre part only when using small saucepans

a warming drawer

a rotisserie for open-spit roasting

rollers or wheels for moving the cooker when cleaning

TI CREDA LTD

a fluorescent hob light

a digital autotimer and clock

a fan assisted oven—this saves electricity by heating up quickly and giving an even temperature

a glass-panelled external door or an inner glass door

double ovens—the smaller oven can be used for normal cooking and the larger oven for large-scale batch baking

self-cleaning oven liners

fast-heating rings

an eye-level dual circuit grill

Another new development is the ceramic hob which can be found on some free-standing electric cookers and built-in electric hobs. The top of the hob is made from a white or black heat-resistant material which completely covers the elements. When the elements are switched on, the circular cooking areas glow red or yellow. A ceramic hob is streamlined in appearance and is very easy to clean. Its flat surface provides another working area, a point worth considering in a small kitchen. Because electric elements retain heat after they have been switched off, the ceramic hob can be dangerous, especially for young children, and spillage from boiling saucepans may run over the whole surface.

When you have found a cooker which suits your needs, fits into your kitchen decor and is the right price, remember to check for design faults.

1 Are switches, handles, knobs and control panels easy to use and in a convenient position? Are they likely to get hot when the oven is switched on? Most manufacturers of electric cookers can supply control panels in braille for the blind.

2 Are there any sharp or protruding features which could be dangerous?

3 Are the cooker surfaces streamlined and easy to clean? Look out for dirt traps.

4 Remember that large areas of chrome look attractive but need constant polishing.

5 Check that there will be plenty of room in your kitchen for the oven door to open completely. Would a left or right hung door be better?

6 Has it been approved by Consumer Protection bodies? (Look for British Gas approval for a gas cooker and BEAB approval for an electric appliance.)

A microwave oven cooks food by electromagnetic short-length, high-frequency radio waves. The microwave energy is absorbed by the food, causing the food molecules to vibrate rapidly against each other. This produces the heat which cooks the food. A microwave oven is an expensive piece of kitchen equipment, but it has many advantages.

1 It speeds up the cooking process. This saves electricity and time.

2 It can be used for defrosting and cooking frozen food taken straight from the freezer.

3 Food cooked in a microwave oven keeps its natural colour and flavour.

4 The important vitamins and mineral salts are not destroyed.

5 There is very little shrinkage of food and no unpleasant cooking smells.

6 Although a microwave oven looks small it has a large capacity and can be used for joints of meat and poultry, as well as smaller dishes such as steaks, sausages and chops.

7 It can roast, boil, steam, bake, poach and grill food.

8 There is no radiant heat so the cooker remains cool. This means that it is easy to wipe clean, and spilled food does not burn on to the cooker. Because the cooker is always cool to the touch there is no danger to young children or elderly people.

9 A microwave oven can be plugged into a 13 or 15 amp power point. This means that it can be moved about when necessary and can be used wherever there is a suitable socket.

10 There is less washing up because saucepans are not needed. The light containers which are needed for microwave cooking make this method suitable for the elderly and the disabled.

11 A microwave oven automatically switches itself off when the door is opened.

There are some disadvantages to microwave cooking. Food is not browned on the outside. If a dish looks too insipid it may have to be finished off under a grill or in an oven. Some microwave ovens have special browning attachments which can be bought separately.

A microwave oven can be noisy in use, and condensation collects inside and outside the oven. Because of the dangers from leaking radiation it is important to check that a microwave oven has passed the British Standard safety tests.

Refrigerators/freezers and larder-fridges

A refrigerator is an attractive and compact alternative to the old-fashioned ventilated larder and cold slab. As well as keeping perishable foods fresh for a short period, a refrigerator cuts down on shopping time and reduces wastage of left-over food. Ready-frozen foods can be stored in the freezer compartment inside the refrigerator. This means that meals can be made in a hurry and that there is always food available in an emergency. The star rating sign on the freezer compartment indicates the length of time frozen foods can be stored.

✳	*up to a week*
✳ ✳	*up to a month*
✳ ✳ ✳	*up to 3 months*
✳ [✳ ✳ ✳]	*will freeze fresh and cooked food and store it for long periods*

The modern refrigerator has ample storage space inside and is designed to work efficiently and economically. It has an elegant, streamlined appearance with wipe-clean surfaces inside and out. There is a variety of shapes, sizes and colours to link up with other kitchen furniture. A refrigerator can fit under standard-height working surfaces, fit flush against other kitchen units, be stacked on top or at the side of freezers, be built in to units or be free-standing.

The amount of food which can be stored in a refrigerator is measured in cubic feet or litres. Sizes for household models range from about 1.75 cu. ft (50 litres) for the very small table top refrigerator to 12.1 cu. ft (343 litres) for a family-size model. Here are some of the features available on a modern refrigerator. Look at the list and discuss which extras you think are essential and which ones are worth paying more for.

continuous automatic defrost mechanism

a cold drinks dispenser

thermostatic temperature control

a coloured finish

a reversible door which can be adjusted to open from the left or right

salad crisper or drawer

adjustable feet

adjustable, hinged or gated shelves for bottles, jugs etc.

ELECTROLUX LTD

fitted shelves inside the door

magnetic door seal

moulded egg storage trays

interior light

scratch resistant worktop

decor panels and trims on the door to match other kitchen equipment

ice-cube trays and extra storage compartment for cubes

A freezer can be used for the long-term storage of fresh fruit, vegetables, meat, fish, cooked dishes and ready-frozen foods. Owning a freezer allows you to buy food when it is in season and therefore at its cheapest. This saves money and also cuts down on shopping time. Freezing home-grown produce and baking in bulk are two ways of using a freezer sensibly. It is also possible to plan for parties, school holidays and the unexpected guest in advance by having a selection of different dishes stored in the freezer.

There are two types of freezer. An upright model has a front opening and takes up little floor space in a kitchen. It has shelves or baskets which make it easy to unload and load food. A chest freezer has a top opening lid, takes up more floor space than an upright model and does not have any shelves. A chest freezer is usually cheaper to buy than an upright freezer and it is useful for storing large bulky items.

The frozen food storage capacity of freezers can vary from 2 cu. ft (56.6 litres) for a tiny upright freezer which can be stacked on top of an upright refrigerator, to about 18.1 cu. ft (512 litres) for a large chest model. Here are some of the features available on upright and chest freezers. Look at the list and discuss which extras you think are essential and which ones are worth paying more for.

ELECTROLUX LTD

flap down shelf fronts for easy loading and unloading

an adjustable thermostat

a fast freeze compartment

pull-out non-tip drawers or shelves for easy storage

interior light

ice trays and storage bin (some expensive models have a dispenser for ice and iced water on the outside of the cabinet)

magnetic door seal

decor panels and trims

an economy switch to cut down on running costs

eye-level controls

frozen food storage guide on inner surface of door

laminated worktop

a reversible door which can be adjusted to open from the left or right

a drainage plug for defrosting (some expensive models do not need defrosting because ice never forms on the inside of the cabinet)

adjustable feet

a red warning light or buzzer to indicate that the temperature inside the freezer has risen a drainage plug for defrosting

a fast freeze compartment

adjustable thermostat

storage baskets and space dividers

rollers for easy movement

a lock and key so that freezers which are housed in a garage or utility room are burglarproof

interior light

a counterbalanced lid to hold it in position when loading and unloading the freezer

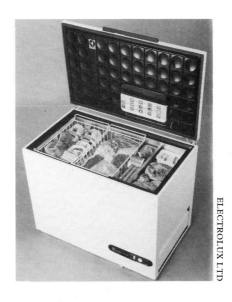

ELECTROLUX LTD

special hinges so that a chest freezer can be opened when it is flush against a wall

a frozen food storage guide on inner surface of lid

magnetic door seal

an economy switch to cut down on running costs

a recessed plinth at the bottom to allow you to stand close when loading and unloading the freezer

a red warning light or buzzer to indicate that the temperature inside the freezer has risen

A fridge/freezer is a sensible arrangement for a small, modern kitchen. It consists of a matching refrigerator and upright freezer stacked one above the other, but only taking up the same amount of floor space as a single appliance.

The larder- or coolstore-fridge is a comparatively new development. It is designed for the freezer owner who does not need a separate frozen food compartment in the refrigerator. The larder-fridge has, therefore, more internal storage space than an ordinary refrigerator. Some models have a cold drinks dispenser as an extra feature.

When you have found a refrigerator and/or freezer which is the right size and type to suit your needs, remember to check for any design faults.

1 Are switches, handles, knobs and control panels easy to use and in a convenient position?

2 Is the machine quiet when working, and free from vibration?

3 Can internal fittings be removed easily for cleaning? Are there any awkward ledges or knobs which will collect dirt? Are external surfaces streamlined and easy to clean? Avoid models which have large areas of chrome or plastic trims because they will need constant polishing.

4 Is defrosting easy? Is the drainage plug in a sensible position so that a bucket or bowl can be placed underneath?
5 Has it been BEAB approved?

Washing machines

The two most popular types of washing machine are the fully automatic model and the twin-tub.

A fully automatic washing machine can be loaded and then programmed to wash, rinse and spin the washing. The complete laundering cycle proceeds automatically without any further attention. Most automatic washing machines will spin clothes leaving them slightly damp. A few automatic washing machines have a tumble drier all-in-one, and these machines get clothes absolutely dry.

An automatic washing machine has a selection of programmes to cope with the different types of fabric. Some models have as many as 22 programmes and can tackle any washing problem from heavily soiled cottons to delicate silk fabrics. It is important to check that the washing machine you intend to buy has enough programmes to cope with the range of clothes you will be washing. Most automatic washing machines take a load of about 5 kg (11 lb) of dry clothes. Some models have an economy feature which can be used for small loads and this saves water, detergent and electricity. An automatic washer can be filled with hot or cold water. It is better to plumb the machine into the domestic water supply. This leaves the taps free for other purposes and also saves time in connecting and disconnecting the filler hoses.

If a separate tumble drier is required it is a good idea to choose a matching model which can be stacked on top or at the side of the washing machine. Some tumble driers are wall mounted and have colourful decorative panels to match other kitchen units.

An automatic washing machine is expensive to buy but it can be a very good investment for a busy, working family. Here are some of the features available on automatic washing machines. Look at the list and discuss which extras you think are essential and which would be worth paying more for.

TI CREDA LTD

safety features to prevent the door from being opened while the machine is working

a dispenser for detergent and fabric conditioner

a drip-dry cycle

a laminated worktop

lights to indicate what stage the machine has reached

a pre-wash soak feature

a wide selection of automatic wash programmes

a cool tumble or slow spin feature for delicate fabrics

HOTPOINT LTD

a rinse and hold feature to keep the washed clothes in clear water until the final spin

an economy wash programme for small loads

separate washing and drying timers

a large porthole for easy front loading and unloading

a filter to trap fluff, threads and loose buttons

thermostatically controlled washing and drying temperatures

a buzzer to indicate when clothes are dry or the wash cycle is complete

electronic controls with fewer moving parts, to make servicing easier

a reverse tumbling action to prevent creasing and tangling

HOTPOINT LTD

A twin-tub washing machine is cheaper to buy than an automatic, but it takes up more space in the kitchen. Clothes have to be transferred by hand from the wash tub to the spinning compartment. A twin-tub will take a wash load of about 3 kg (6·5 lb) of dry clothes. It cuts washing time to a minimum because two loads of clothes can be treated simultaneously, one load in the wash tub and the other in the spin drier. This makes it useful for families whose large varied wash would require several different wash cycles in an automatic machine.

Here are some design features to look for when choosing a washing machine or tumble drier.

1 Will loading and unloading the machine be easy?

2 Is the machine quiet when working, and free from vibration?

3 Are control knobs, handles and switches firmly fixed and at a convenient height? Are they easy to use?

4 Has the machine any sharp features which could be dangerous, or has it any awkward ledges to trap dirt? Are external surfaces streamlined and easy to clean?

5 Check that a free-standing tumble drier or a twin-tub washing machine has rollers so that it can be moved about the kitchen easily.

6 Can a twin-tub be emptied easily?

7 Has the machine been BEAB approved?

Dishwashers

A dishwasher is not an essential piece of kitchen equipment but it can be extremely useful for a busy working family. It saves time, hot water and detergent, and does away with the dull, repetitive task of washing up all the dirty dishes after each meal.

The most economical way to use a dishwasher is to accumulate a full load of dirty crockery before switching the machine on. This means that a family must have sufficient crockery and cutlery to last a full day, and must have a dishwasher big enough to take about twelve place settings. A dishwasher gives extra storage space in the kitchen because everyday items, which are being used continually, can be left in the machine after being washed until they are required for the next meal.

There are many different designs of dishwasher. Some models stand on worktops or draining boards. Others are floor models and are designed to fit either under a work surface or with their own worktop. Some dishwashers are fixed to a wall at a convenient height so that there is no need to bend down when loading and unloading the machine. Most dishwashers have a pull-down front door, and it is important to check that there is sufficient room in the kitchen to open the door completely.

The interior surface of a dishwasher can be made of stainless steel or polypropylene. Both materials are hard wearing and long lasting. Stainless steel does not scratch or stain and is self-cleaning, but polypropylene is better at cutting down sound vibration. Some models have a polyurethane foam jacket which makes the machine quieter when in use.

Here are some of the special features available on dishwashers. Look at the list and decide which extras you think are essential and which are worth paying more for.

adjustable drawers or baskets for large items, such as saucepans, roasting tins, casseroles

a separate cutlery section with a small mesh or solid base to stop the cutlery falling through

a rinse and hold feature so that items can be rinsed after use, and then left until a full load is ready to be washed

a half-load and plate-warming sequence—people who like to wash up after each meal should choose a model with a short cycle wash

a filter to collect food debris

HOTPOINT LTD

an automatic water softener to prevent lime building up on the heating element

a selection of wash programmes to cater for delicate items, normal loads and very dirty dishes—some machines have 6 or 7 washing sequences

removable spray arms so that jets can be cleaned

a feature to reduce water pressure when washing fine china or glass

a childproof door with a safety mechanism to ensure that the machine cannot be opened whilst it is operating

a rinse-aid dispenser to prevent streaks on glassware

When choosing a dishwasher, remember to check for any design faults.

1 Are the controls easy to use and in a convenient position? Look for neat push-button knobs, and indicators which show clearly the programme which has been selected.

2 Are there any sharp features which could be dangerous?

3 Is the appliance fitted with adjustable feet for uneven surfaces, and are there wheels or slides so that floor models can be moved for cleaning?

4 Are there any indicators to show when the water softener and rinse-aid compartments need refilling?

5 Does the position of the hose allow the appliance to be used to the right or left of the sink?

6 Can the dishwasher be plumbed into the water supply to leave the taps free?

7 Is the machine quiet when in use?

8 Has the machine been BEAB approved?

Vacuum cleaners

An electric vacuum cleaner sucks up loose dirt. It is an efficient, labour-saving device which is capable of cleaning a variety of household surfaces.

There are three main types:

the cylinder vacuum cleaner

the upright vacuum cleaner

the canister vacuum cleaner

The cylinder and canister models are light and easy to manoeuvre. Some actually slide on a cushion of air. They clean mainly by suction and have filters to trap dirt so that the air remains fresh. They are less expensive to buy than upright vacuum cleaners.

An upright vacuum cleaner has a motor which drives a series of brushes. The brushes beat the carpet, loosening any dust and dirt, which is then sucked up by the cleaner. The brushes can be adjusted to suit different piles and surfaces. An upright vacuum cleaner is easier to store than a cylinder or canister model. There is usually a kit of attachments which includes a crevice tool, upholstery brush, carpet/floor nozzle, flexible hose and telescopic extension tube. These attachments are useful for cleaning different surfaces, but since they are bought separately it is worth considering whether they are really necessary.

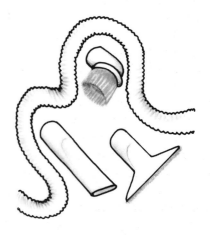

Nearly all vacuum cleaners have a disposable inner bag which can be re-used several times.

When choosing a vacuum cleaner try out a few different models to see which you like best. Look for a model which is easy to use and is efficient at cleaning a variety of surfaces. Check for any design faults.

1 Is the cleaner light to handle and easy to manoeuvre? Are attachments easy to assemble?

2 Are the control knobs/switches in a sensible position?

3 Will the vacuum clean right up to the skirting board, and are there any sharp features which might scratch woodwork and furniture?

4 Does the model look attractive?

5 Has it any awkward crevices which will collect dirt?

6 Is it quiet when being used?

7 Can the cord be rewound and stored easily? Are the attachments bulky to store?

8 Is it easy to disconnect and empty the inner dust bag?

9 Has the model been BEAB approved?

Food mixers

There are two types of food mixer:

    a the lightweight hand mixer;

    b the heavier table model.

A hand-held model usually has two beaters and a set of whisks. It can be used for a variety of mixing jobs, e.g. creaming fat and sugar, whisking eggs, whipping cream, mashing potatoes and beating batters. Because a hand mixer is light and portable, it can be used anywhere in the kitchen. This means that it can be used on the cooker hob if a mixing process requires heat.

A table mixer consists of a mixing bowl and stand. It usually has a pair of beaters, a whisk and a spatula. Extra attachments, such as a dough hook, a juice extractor, a slicer and shredder, a mincer and liquidizer, can be bought separately. This type of food mixer is heavier and more expensive than a hand model. Each of the processes requires the stand so this means that the mixer cannot be used on a cooker hob. If a food mixer does not have a liquidizing attachment, it may be useful to buy a separate liquidizer or blender for making soups, drinks, purées and baby foods.

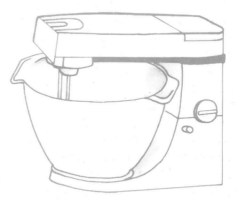

A food mixer does save time and energy, but because it is expensive to buy, uses electricity and makes extra washing up it may not be a sensible purchase unless there are large quantities of food to cope with.

Here are some design features to check for when choosing a food mixer.

1 Is the machine easy to use? Are handles and switches in a convenient position?

2 Does the mixer do its job efficiently?

3 Can the machine be used at different speeds?

4 Is the machine quiet when switched on?

5 Are the various attachments easy to fix, use, remove and clean?

6 Is the mixer streamlined? Look for sharp features and awkward dust traps.

7 Will the machine and attachments be bulky and difficult to store? Some models have special wall brackets for easy storage.

8 Has the model been BEAB approved?

Electric slow cookers

An electric slow cooker cooks food slowly and gently, and makes tasty soups, stews and pot roasts from cheap cuts of meat. This type of slow cooker is ideal for a busy working family. It can be switched on in the morning and left to cook slowly through the day without boiling dry. It uses very little electricity and is more economical than a conventional cooker.

Some models have a high and low heat setting, and a removable earthenware inner bowl which can be totally immersed when washing up. This type is much easier to wash than the one piece model which has to be handled carefully to avoid getting the electrical socket wet.

Kettles

A well-designed kettle is attractive and practical to use. It should have a streamlined appearance, with no awkward lips or ledges which will collect dirt. The handle and knob should be heat-resistant and easy to grasp. The lid should be tightly fitting with no dangerously placed steam vents to scald the holder, and the spout should pour well. A kettle which is placed on a gas or electric burner should have a flat, sturdy base. Some models have a heat-absorbing coil in the bottom to heat the water rapidly, and a whistle to indicate when boiling point has been reached .

An electric automatic kettle switches itself off when the water boils. It can be reset by pressing a button. Some models have a warning buzzing mechanism or light to

A slow cooker is attractive enough to be taken straight to the dining table when serving meals. This saves time and washing up.

TI TOWER HOUSEWARES LTD

TI RUSSELL HOBBS LTD

indicate when the water has boiled. A well-designed automatic kettle has the element set low so that small quantities of water can be boiled economically. Other design features which are available on more expensive models are:

a a seamless base to prevent leaking;

b a wide spout so that the kettle can be filled through the spout or lid;

c a body which is moulded in a stay-cool plastic material;

d an indicator which shows how full of water the kettle is;

e a coloured and patterned enamel body.

Saucepans

Saucepans can be made from aluminium, enamelled aluminium, enamelled steel, aluminium with a copper coating, stainless steel with an aluminium base or stainless steel with a copper base. Some saucepans, casseroles and frying pans are coated with a special plastic called polytetrafluorethylene (PTFE) to prevent cooked foods from sticking. "Teflon" and "Tefal" are familiar trade names for non-stick cooking utensils.

When choosing saucepans, buy the best you can afford. Heavy pans will usually last longer than flimsy light ones. Look for:

a a solid flat base (this type is suitable for gas or electric cookers);

b a sturdy heat-resistant handle and knob (which are comfortable to hold);

c a tightly-fitting lid (if there are steam control vents check that they are not in a dangerous position);

d a non-stick interior;

e an easily-cleaned exterior;

f a pan which will pour easily (a shaped lip is an advantage, especially for a milk saucepan).

TI TOWER HOUSEWARES LTD

Some models have detachable handles. This means that the saucepans can be stacked inside each other when not in use. This saves space in the kitchen. They can also be used as "freezer" casseroles (snap-on plastic lids are sometimes provided), or taken directly to the table as serving dishes. If you wish to use saucepans as casseroles for oven baking, choose a design which has two handles. This type is easier to carry. Remember that the handles, knobs and fittings must be of an ovenproof material.

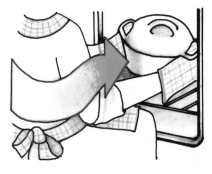

Electric irons and ironing boards

Electric irons are thermostatically controlled and have easy-to-use heat selectors or fabric guides. There are three main types of iron:

a the steam spray iron;

b the steam dry iron;

c the dry iron.

Most steam irons can be used either dry or filled with water. The water comes out as steam and helps to remove creases when pressing garments. Steam spray irons have a press-button action which releases an extra spray or jet of steam to deal with very stubborn creases. Steam irons should be easy to fill. Some models have transparent, removable water reservoirs, and special valves to prevent fur deposits forming in hard water areas. Dry irons are usually heavier to handle than steam irons, and the extra weight helps to give a good finish.

When choosing an iron, look for a model which:

a. *is comfortable to hold;*
b. *feels the right weight;*
c. *has a sharply-pointed tip for getting into awkward corners and gathers;*
d. *has easy-to-operate control switches.*

HOTPOINT LTD

Ironing boards can be made from steel or wood. They should have sturdy legs with non-slip feet, and be easy to assemble and collapse. Most ironing boards can be adjusted to different height positions, but before buying any particular model check to see if it can be adjusted to a comfortable height for you. If you like to iron whilst sitting down, make certain that there is room for your legs to fit under the table.

There should be a rest for the iron at one end. This can be made of non-flaking asbestos, a sheet of stainless steel or thin strips of metal, but look to see if there is a raised rim to prevent the iron from slipping off the rest.

Ironing boards should have a well-padded surface. This is usually made of foam with a removable cotton cover. Some foam-backed covers have a metallized finish which helps to reflect heat. These covers are stain-resistant and water-repellant.

Television and sound equipment

When choosing television or sound equipment, it is important to get expert advice. Read the relevant articles in "Which?", and study the performance ratings of the various models. Look at recommended "best buys", and check their design features. Here are some general points to consider.

1 Does it look attractive? Will it fit in with your furniture and interior decoration?

2 Are the controls simple to use and in a sensible position? Will they be easy to keep clean? Remember that large areas of metal or plastic will show dust, dirt and fingermarks.

3 Check the amount of power the equipment uses. A low-powered model will be more economical to run than one which is high-powered.

4 Look for a long mains flex. This makes it easy to manoeuvre. If you are choosing a portable television or record player, check that it has a sturdy carrying handle.

5 Look for BEAB approval. Check that a television set has passed flammability tests, and look to see that any holes or slots in the back cover are very small, so that it is impossible to touch live parts when the set is switched on.

If you decide to buy television or sound equipment from an electrical discount warehouse, ask about their after-sales service. Some discount firms only service equipment which is returned to them, and some have a call-out fee even when an item is still under guarantee.

Many families decide to rent a television set rather than buy it outright. This means that they continue to pay a rent for as long as they keep the set. Renting a television usually works out more expensive than buying it, but it must be remembered that if a fault develops the television will be repaired or replaced free of charge by the rental firm. Buying a television means that there is a large initial expense and the possibility of subsequent repair bills, but the set becomes the property of the buyer and can be re-sold or used in part-exchange for a new model. Television and sound equipment can be bought on credit terms so that the cost can be spread over a period of years.

Think and Do

1. In your own words describe the differences between:
a. a freezer and a refrigerator;
b. a tumble drier and a spin drier;
c. a steam iron and a dry iron;
d. an upright vacuum cleaner and a cylinder vacuum cleaner;
e. British Gas approval and BEAB approval.
2. List some of the advantages and disadvantages of owning:
a. an automatic washing machine;
b. a dishwasher.
3. Say what is meant by each of the following:
a. a flame failure device on a gas cooker;
b. dual circuit rings on an electric cooker;
c. self-cleaning oven liners;
d. a cooker autotimer;
e. a ceramic hob.
4. Copy the diagram of refrigerator star rating signs (page 103) into your notebook. What features would you look for when buying a small free-standing refrigerator?
5. Look around your kitchen at home and make a list of the "hidden" dangers or problems which would face:
a. a left-handed person;
b. a disabled person in a wheelchair;
c. old people.
6. Give some general advice on buying electrical appliances. Choose one particular washing machine or television set and:
a. find out the recommended list price;
b. find out where you could get the best discount price in your area (but remember to add on any extra charges);
c. calculate the difference between the discount price of the appliance and the amount it would cost to buy the same appliance on credit terms.

7. Look through advertising leaflets, mail order catalogues or magazines and find a picture of a kitchen appliance. Stick it into your notebook. Underneath the picture answer the following questions.

a. Do you like the appearance of the appliance? Say why you like or dislike it.

b. Do you think it will do its job well? Give reasons for your answer.

c. Can you suggest any improvements which might be made to the design of the appliance?

d. Which safety features, if any, make it suitable for families with young children?

8. Find out the current prices of:

a. a twin-tub washing machine;

b. a free-standing electric cooker with a fan-assisted oven;

c. disposable inner dust bags for an upright vacuum cleaner;

d. an electric casserole with a removable inner bowl;

e. a lightweight hand food mixer;

f. a good quality whistling kettle;

g. a "Teflon" coated frying pan;

h. a replacement ironing board cover with a metallized finish.

9. What points would you look for when choosing:

a. an ironing board;

b. a set of saucepans;

c. a kettle?

10. Look at the picture of an oven and then answer the following questions.

a. What type of oven is it?

b. How does it cook food?

c. List some of the disadvantages of cooking food in this way.

d. What are the advantages of this type of oven?

TOSHIBA (UK) LTD

The design of manufactured products

Tableware

Modern tableware is made from three kinds of pottery.

1 Earthenware is a cheap pottery which is used for everyday tableware. It is fired at a low temperature. Rough earthenware is porous and cannot be used to hold liquids until it is "glazed". Decoration can be applied under the glaze or on top of it. If a glaze is chipped or cracked, the dull, porous clay underneath will absorb moisture, so chipped earthenware should be discarded.

2 Stoneware is a hard and strong pottery which is made from coarse clay. It is fired at a very high temperature and forms a dull grey or brown pottery. Stoneware is not porous so it does not need to be glazed. Stoneware is used to make oven-to-tableware, a very strong pottery which is resistant to chips and scratches, and is unaffected by heat.

3 Porcelain is a very fine and delicate pottery. It is expensive to buy so is more suitable for "best" dinner and tea services. Porcelain is fired at a very high temperature and is brilliant white. It is translucent which means that light can be seen through it. **Bone china** is made from an artificial porcelain, consisting of a mixture of ox-bone ash, china stone, and china clay or kaolin. Bone china looks fragile but is very strong and does not chip easily.

There are so many attractive styles and patterns of pottery, that choosing tableware can be difficult. It is wise to limit your choice by deciding whether you need "everyday" crockery which is hard-wearing (earthenware or stoneware would be suitable), or expensive fine porcelain which will have to be handled with care.

Today's designs in stoneware are extremely elegant making them suitable for all occasions from everyday use to special dinner parties. They are oven-, freezer- and dishwasher-safe, and are chip-resistant and hard wearing so should last for years.

Well-designed tableware is simple in shape and decoration. It has clean, sleek lines which are attractive and practical. Surfaces are smooth and flat. Handles on cups, jugs, lids and serving dishes are well formed and comfortable to hold. Lips and spouts pour without dripping and have wide necks which are easy to clean. There are no unnecessary ridges or ledges to collect dirt. Cups sit squarely in saucers, and jugs, tea and coffee pots have wide bases which make them firm and difficult to tip over. Here are some examples of well-designed tableware.

"Cornrose" by Hornsea

"Contrast" by Hornsea

"Gypsy" by Denby

"Fieldflower" by Royal Doulton

It is a good idea to buy matching dinner and tea services. This means that pieces can be interchanged, a useful point to consider when camouflaging breakages. Choose a well-known design which is not likely to be discontinued for a number of years, so that extra or replacement items can be bought when necessary. If you have a dishwasher, do check that the tableware you buy is dishwasher-safe, and always use a recommended detergent in the machine.

It is possible to buy tableware rejects from factory shops, "seconds" shops and market stalls. The fault may just be a slight flaw in the pattern. These reject pieces can be bargains if you buy sensibly, but always avoid tableware which is chipped, scratched or cracked.

Glassware

Ordinary glass is made from a mixture of silica, sodium oxide and calcium oxide. Expensive lead crystal has red lead added to produce a fine lustre and brilliance, which glistens like diamonds when it is cut. Heat-resistant glassware, such as Pyrex, contains mainly silica and borax. This makes a glass which expands very little when it is heated, and so is safe to use in an oven.

Most household glass is blown or pressed into shape by machinery, but some expensive pieces of lead crystal are still shaped and cut by hand. Machine-made glass can be washed in a dishwasher, but hand-made glass is too delicate. It should be washed carefully by hand to preserve its fine lustre.

Well-designed glassware is simple, elegant and well proportioned. It can have sleek, curved lines or a solid "chunky" shape, but it should be comfortable to hold and to drink from, and feel balanced when it is held in the hand. Stems should be plain and sturdy with firm bases which are not easy to tip over. Glasses with ornately shaped stems can be difficult to wash and dry. Surfaces should be smooth and free from flaws or bubbles. Hand-made glasses may, however, have one or two flaws. This is difficult to avoid. The tops of drinking glasses, water jugs and vases should not be too narrow or washing and drying will be difficult.

It is sensible to choose simple, sturdy goblets for everyday use. Select a range which can be bought separately, so that breakages can be replaced easily. If you decide to start collecting lead crystal glasses for special occasions, choose a well-known range which is not likely to be discontinued. This will allow you to add to your collection over a period of years. Here are some examples of well-designed glassware.

"Star of Edinburgh" by Edinburgh Crystal

"Apollo" by Ravenhead

"Siesta" by Ravenhead

"London" by Thomas Webb Crystal

Cutlery

Modern cutlery can be made from stainless steel, silver, silver plate or bronze. A steel which will not corrode, rust or tarnish is formed by the addition of chromium and nickel. Stainless steel is a popular metal for cutlery because it is hard, does not lose its shine, and is very easy to clean. Silver is a precious metal which can be used to make very expensive pieces of tableware and cutlery. Because it is so expensive most "silver" cutlery is only plated with the metal. Silver plate is called electro-plated nickel silver and should be marked with the letters E.P.N.S. Bronze is made from copper and tin. It is a hard metal which does not corrode or tarnish easily. Solid bronze cutlery is very expensive to buy.

Cutlery handles can be made from the same metal as the blades, or they can be shaped from other materials such as wood, horn, nylon, mother of pearl, plastics or ceramics (baked clay).

Well-designed cutlery is comfortable to hold and fits snugly in the hand. Knife and fork handles should have curved ends which do not dig into the palms, and there should be no sharp ridges to cause discomfort. Fork prongs should be gently pointed to pierce food efficiently, but should not be too close together because this makes cleaning difficult. The bowl of a spoon should be fairly deep. If it is too shallow it will not scoop up food. The edges of the bowl should be smooth and well finished. Any sharp features might cut the inside of the mouth. Knife blades should be flat and straight with one strong cutting edge. A steak knife has a serrated blade to cut cleanly through meat. The joint between the blade and handle should be very firm. If you use a dishwasher do check to see that the cutlery handles are dishwasher-safe.

Modern cutlery is not only functional, it is extremely attractive. Designs are less elaborate than they used to be and patterns are simple and sleek.

Cutlery can be bought as individual items, as place settings or as a canteen in a presentation box. Here are some examples of well-designed cutlery.

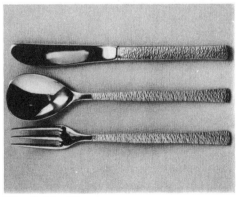

"Studio" by Viners

"Love Story" by Viners

"Nordic" by Viners

Plastic household products
Synthetic plastics are manufactured from chemicals found in substances like crude oil, petroleum and coal. They are widely used to make household products, utensils and fittings.

Polythene is a well-known synthetic plastic which can be shaped as bowls, buckets, waste bins, storage containers, and kitchen, bathroom and garden tools. Polythene products can be soft and flexible like a "squeezy" detergent bottle, or hard and rigid like a washing-up bowl. They will not break, chip or rust. Polythene products are easy to clean, quiet in use, light in weight, very tough and hard wearing, and available in a range of colours.

When choosing plastic household items look for simple shapes which will be functional as well as attractive. Handles should be firm, easy to grasp and comfortable to hold. Surfaces should be smooth and free from dirt-collecting ridges. Lids should snap on tightly but be simple to remove. Containers should have wide tops for easy access, and products such as bowls, sieves, colanders, buckets and storage bins should be seamless for easy cleaning.

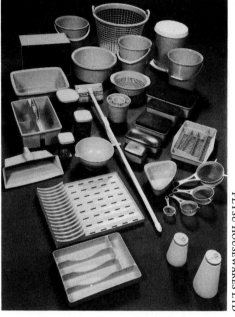

PLYSU HOUSEWARES LTD

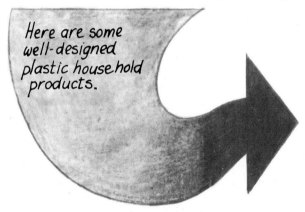

Here are some well-designed plastic household products.

Toys

Toys made in this country have to pass the British Standards Institution safety tests but many toys made abroad are not so durable or safe. Always be wary of cheap, imported plastic toys. They may:

a break, splinter or shatter easily;

b be made from toxic (poisonous) materials such as infected stuffing, lead paint, dangerous chemicals and dyes;

    c be badly constructed and fall apart to reveal lethal nails, sharp internal mechanisms, rough surfaces and loose pieces which can be swallowed, inhaled or pushed into ears or noses.

    Here are some points to look for when choosing toys.

1 Choose strong, well-made toys which are suitable for the age of a child and the stage of his growth and development.

2 Check that any paint, dye, lacquer or stuffing material is non-toxic.

3 Materials and fillings should be non-inflammable.

4 Folding mechanisms should be childproof, and any clock-work mechanism should be completely enclosed. Operating levers and buttons should be chunky and easy to manipulate.

5 Wheeled toys should be stable and easy to steer.

6 Soft toys should have screw-in eyes, and legs and arms which will not pull out.

7 Electric motors should not exceed 24 volts.

8 Check that there are no sharp edges which could cut or scratch and no detachable pieces which could be swallowed.

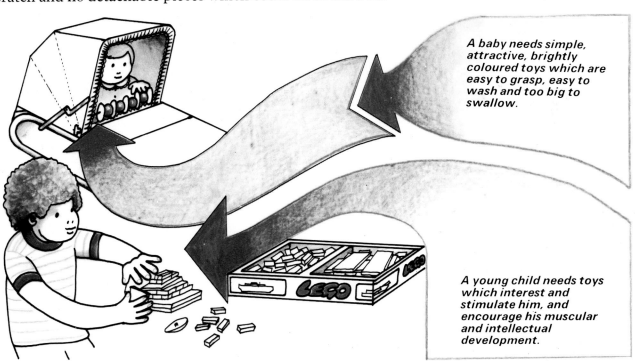

A baby needs simple, attractive, brightly coloured toys which are easy to grasp, easy to wash and too big to swallow.

A young child needs toys which interest and stimulate him, and encourage his muscular and intellectual development.

Here are some well-designed toys by Fisher-Price Toys.

Push-along clown

Lift and load depot

A shape-posting box

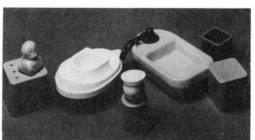

A tub tug and barge set

Think and Do

1. List some of the advantages and disadvantages of buying tableware rejects.

2. Here is a popular design of tableware by Hornsea Pottery Co. Ltd called "Tapestry". Draw, colour and name your own design for a matching cup, saucer and plate.

3. Make a study of *one* of the following:

a. tableware for young children;

b. tableware and eating aids for the physically handicapped;

c. disposable tableware for picnics and parties.

4. Find out the names of the following:

a. a firm which is famous for making hand-cut lead crystal;

b. a British and a German firm which are famous for porcelain;

c. a trade name which you associate with the "Potteries";

d. a British city which is famous for stainless steel cutlery;

e. an area in Britain where china clay is mined;

f. a Scandinavian country which is famous for its modern designs in glass and stainless steel.

5. Are these sentences *true* or *false*?

a. Rough stoneware is porous.

b. Bone ash is used to make bone china.

c. Another name for silver plate is electro-plated nickel silver.

d. Porcelain is transparent.

e. Silica and borax are used to make heat-resistant glass.

f. Polythene is a common synthetic plastic.

g. Bronze is made from copper and stainless steel.

h. Stoneware is used to make oven-to-tableware.

6. Make a study of the toys available in your local shops. Do you think they are all well designed? List some points to remember when buying toys.

7. What points would you look for when choosing:

a. cutlery;

b. wine glasses;

c. a plastic measuring jug;

d. a tea or coffee pot;

e. ovenproof serving dishes;

f. salad servers?

8. Visit your school and local libraries and find out all you can about *one* of the following:

a. how pottery is shaped, fired, glazed and decorated;

b. how glass is made, shaped and decorated;

c. how synthetic plastics are manufactured.

9. The following are famous makes of tableware. Name them.

a. WGODEODEW;

b. YNEDB;

c. SERAHON;

d. DEPOS;

e. KANMIE;

f. YLARO LUNDOTO;

g. NWROC RYBED;

h. DIRMWTEIN.

10. Find out the current prices of:

a. a set of Pyrex mixing bowls;

b. six steak knives;

c. a stainless steel vegetable dish;

d. a small cut-glass vase;

e. a polythene washing up bowl;

f. six "everyday" cereal bowls;

g. six E.P.N.S. teaspoons;

h. a plastic colander.

The design of soft furnishings

Soft furnishings are the accessories which help to make rooms comfortable and attractive, such as curtains, cushions, chair covers, bed linen and table linen. It is important to choose suitable fabrics for each of these furnishings so that they are durable and useful. Here is a guide showing soft furnishing materials.

Material	Advantages/Disadvantages	Where suitable
Cotton, cotton blends, e.g. cotton/viscose, cotton/polyester, cotton/nylon, cotton/terylene	Can be plain or patterned; available in different finishes, e.g. denim, corduroy; hard wearing; attractive; easy to wash and iron; can be crease- and stain-resistant.	Curtains, curtain linings, bed sheets, bedspreads, duvet covers, tea towels, tablecloths, place mats, napkins
Linen, linen blends, e.g. linen/cotton, linen/polyester	Tough, long-lasting and absorbent; pure linen requires starching and is expensive; linen blends are cheaper; hard wearing and attractive; easy to launder; can be crease- and stain-resistant.	Tablecloths, place mats, napkins, bed sheets, tea towels
Viscose, viscose blends, e.g. viscose/acetate, viscose/polyester, viscose/nylon	Drape well but soil easily; blends are hard wearing and easy to launder.	Curtains, upholstery fabrics, duvet covers, bedspreads
Triacetate	Easy to launder.	"Candlewick" bedspreads, bathroom mat sets, curtains, cushion covers

Material	Advantages/Disadvantages	Where suitable
Acrylic, acrylic blends, e.g. acrylic/polyester, acrylic/cotton	Resemble wool; feel warm; strong fabrics which are hard wearing; easy to launder.	Curtains, upholstery fabrics, blankets, bedspreads
Modacrylic	Flame-resistant.	Curtains
Nylon	Hard wearing; crease-resistant; easy to launder; non-inflammable; non-absorbent.	Curtains, stretch upholstery covers, tablecloths, place mats, napkins, bed sheets
Polyester	Hard wearing; crease-resistant; easy to launder; soft fabrics which drape well.	Curtains (net and velvet), lace tablecloths, stretch upholstery covers, bedspreads, filling for duvets, pillows and cushions
Glass fibre	Very hard wearing; fire-retardent; drip-dry; non-iron.	Curtains
Leather	Expensive; wears well; warm.	Upholstery fabric
Plastics, e.g. vinyl, PVC, polyurethane, polypropylene	Leather imitations wear well and feel soft; very easy to clean; polyurethane foam burns rapidly and gives off poisonous fumes; polypropylene resists stains.	Upholstery fabrics—polyurethane foam used for furniture fillings
Wool, wool blends, e.g. wool/nylon, wool/viscose, wool/polyester	Wool is warm, hard wearing and does not burn easily; blends are cheaper and hard wearing.	Upholstery fabrics, blankets, filling for duvets, pillows and cushions
Vinyl-coated fabrics	Hard wearing; wipe clean.	Tablecloths, place mats

Bed linen

The continental quilt or duvet has simplified bed-making. It consists of a big bag which is divided into seamed pockets. The pockets are filled with feathers, down, polyester, dacron or a wool/polyester blend. The quilt is protected by a cover which can be removed for washing. A continental quilt can be used without any additional bedding other than a bottom sheet. The quilt hugs the body, giving maximum insulation, and keeps you warm in winter and cool in summer.

Quilt covers, frilled valances, sheets and pillowcases can be bought in a variety of exciting colours and patterns. Plain pastel shades or deep dyed colours can be used to pick out or match the main colour in the bedroom wallpaper, carpet or curtains. Patterned bed linen is available in delicate mini-motifs, simple geometric shapes, patchworks and all-over floral designs. Sets of co-ordinated bed linen often consist of patterned quilt cover and pillowcases, teamed with plain deep dyed sheets and valances. Some designs are available in matching wallpaper, curtains and blinds.

A continental quilt or duvet has a "tog rating" to describe its warmth; the higher the number, the warmer the quilt.

Most modern bed linen is made from cotton/polyester fabrics, which are crease- and stain-resistant, and very hard wearing. They require little or no ironing and are colour-fast. Nylon sheets are cheaper to buy than cotton/polyester. They are easy to wash and dry and do not require ironing, but because nylon is a non-absorbent fibre they can be uncomfortable in warm or hot weather. Nylon sheets are made with a smooth, brushed or non-slip loop finish. Brushed nylon feels warmer and is suitable for winter use. Cotton sheets are cool, comfortable and hard wearing, but they do not have the easy care properties of cotton/polyester or nylon. Cotton bedding can have a plain weave, a hard wearing twill weave, or a fluffed flannelette finish to give extra warmth during winter. Cotton/polyester, nylon and cotton sheets are made in a variety of plain colours and attractive patterns.

Sheets can be flat or fitted. A fitted bottom sheet, which fits snugly over the mattress, keeps the bed looking smooth, and simplifies bed making. Stretch-fitted bottom sheets are made from a cotton/nylon blend. They have a "towelling" finish which makes them soft, absorbent and very comfortable to lie on.

It is possible to buy coloured and patterned sheeting by the metre if you wish to make your own bed linen. This is more economical than buying bedding and it allows you to decorate sheets and pillowcases with contrasting borders, appliqué motifs or bought trims to give them a personal touch.

If blankets are required, buy the best you can afford. Most blankets can be machine-washed and drip-dried. They can be made from pure wool, cotton, a wool/man-made fibre blend, or synthetic fibres such as acrilan, courtelle, polyester and viscose. Wool and wool/man-made blankets should be moth-proofed. Blankets can be bought in a variety of rich colours, and can have hemmed or bound edges. Nylon satin binding is better than rayon because it is hard wearing and will not shrink. Cotton blankets are not as warm or soft as wool but they can be boiled. This makes them useful for young children, old people or the very sick, where frequent washing may be necessary.

When sheets and blankets are used instead of a duvet, the bed linen is usually covered with a bedspread during the

daytime. This can be loose and flat, or fitted to the mattress with side frills or valances. A bedspread can be made of nylon, cotton or a mixture of fibres. A nylon quilt is often placed on top of the bedspread. This looks attractive and gives extra weight, warmth and insulation to the bed linen.

A throwover bedspread or fitted cover is also required if a bed is to be used as a seating unit during the daytime. This should be made of a hard-wearing fabric which can be easily washed. Giant scatter cushions or wedge-shaped pillows arranged against the wall make a comfortable surface to lounge against.

Good quality pillows are soft and resilient, and keep their shape during use. They can be filled with feathers, down, foam rubber, polyester or dacron. Some pillows can be washed by hand, but do check the label first. People who are allergic to feathers or have breathing complaints such as asthma and bronchitis, should choose pillows and quilts which have man-made fillings. These are free from dust.

Table linen

Tablecloths and napkins used to be made from linen, hence the name "table linen". Linen is a strong fabric which launders well and does not hold stains. It is an expensive fabric to buy, and requires starching and ironing to produce its crisp attractive finish. Nowadays, linen has largely been replaced by a range of colourful, easy-care fabrics which are attractive, hard wearing and simple to launder. Synthetic fabrics and blends of natural and synthetic fibres can be machine-washed and drip-dried, and are often resistant to stains and creases.

Table linen is available in a variety of colours, ranging from pale pastel shades to rich deep dyes. Patterns are printed, woven or embossed on the surface of the fabric. Materials with a seersucker finish do not need ironing. Tablecloths are made in square, rectangular and circular shapes, and are often sold in sets with matching napkins. Individual place mats can be made from fabric, woven grasses, plastic or vinyl-coated material. Place mats are versatile and can be used on polished wooden tables for a formal meal, or on formica kitchen surfaces for a snack.

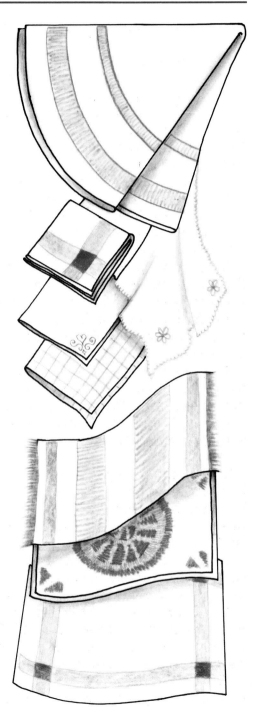

It is very simple to make your own table linen from good-quality dress material. Cotton, linen, nylon, terylene and cotton/man-made blends are suitable, but do check that colours are fast. Choose easy-care fabrics which match your furnishing scheme. If you are making curtains or cushion covers, why not buy extra material for some table linen? Tablecloths should be made the same shape as the table, but should be larger to allow for an all-round overlap of about 20 cm. Place mats should be large enough to take a complete setting of cutlery and crockery. Remember that fabric place mats are not heat-resistant, so they should be used over cork, rush or wooden mats. Vinyl place mats are very practical for families with young children because they can be wiped clean with a damp cloth. Plastic fabrics with a textured surface have to be scrubbed.

Curtains

Curtains help to insulate a room by eliminating draughts from ill-fitting windows. They also deaden noise and protect furniture and furnishings from the fading effect of sunlight. Curtains are often a focal point of a room and can be eye-catching and decorative as well as functional.

Curtains should look attractive open and closed. They should drape in natural folds and look as effective in daylight as in artificial lighting. Patterns should be chosen with care. If a room has a heavily patterned carpet, then plain or textured curtains will be safer. Avoid having too many different patterns in any one room. The result can be restless and confusing. The scale of patterned curtains should be in proportion to the room and size of window. Big repeat patterns suit large areas where the whole pattern can be appreciated. Smaller patterns with mini-repeats are suitable anywhere. Before buying patterned curtaining, drape it in tight folds to see if the pattern will look as effective when the curtains are pushed back.

Curtains can help to create an atmosphere. Smooth, silky fabrics are elegant but cool. Velvets are rich and warm. Textured materials are comfortable and homely.

When choosing curtains look for hard-wearing fabrics which can be machine-washed. If you pick curtains which have to be dry cleaned, this is an added expense. Curtains should be colour-fast and shrink-resistant. Avoid fabrics which will fade. Hessian is a warm fabric but it does lose its colour easily, so only use fabrics like this at windows which do not get much sunshine. Fibreglass curtains have insulating properties. They must be washed by hand and drip-dried. Translucent net curtains are useful if you want privacy in a room without blocking out the light and sunshine. They are also suitable for obscuring an unattractive view. Nylon or polyester net curtains can be teamed with thicker draw curtains which can be closed at night.

Most curtains drape better if they are lined. A lining also protects the curtain fabric from the fading effect of sunlight. Always check that lining material has been pre-shrunk.

Here are some suitable curtain fabrics.

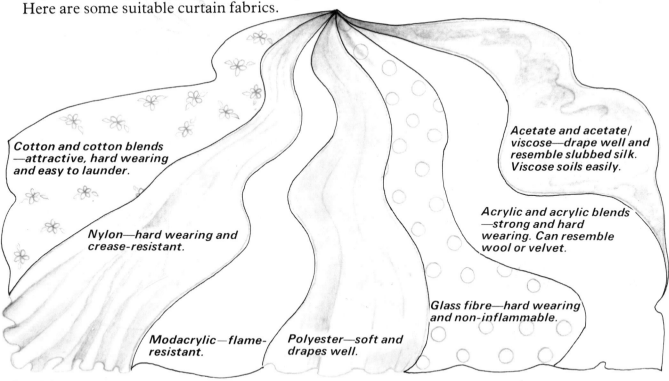

Cotton and cotton blends —attractive, hard wearing and easy to launder.

Nylon—hard wearing and crease-resistant.

Modacrylic—flame-resistant.

Polyester—soft and drapes well.

Glass fibre—hard wearing and non-inflammable.

Acetate and acetate/ viscose—drape well and resemble slubbed silk. Viscose soils easily.

Acrylic and acrylic blends —strong and hard wearing. Can resemble wool or velvet.

Cushions
Cushions are useful accessories in a room. They give comfort and support to your back when you are sitting down and

they add interest, pattern, texture and colour to a decorative scheme.

Round, square or rectangular cushions are popular but shapes such as ovals, triangles, boxes and bolsters look unusual and attractive. Sizes range from tiny "neck" pillows to giant floor cushions or "sag bags". The size of cushions should be governed by the size of the furniture on which they are used. Small, neat cushions suit armchairs, but larger cushions are required for settees and window seats. Groups of scatter cushions made from co-ordinating or toning fabrics look effective on settees.

Almost any kind of material can be used for cushions, from rich velvets to simple cottons. Plain fabrics can be decorated with appliqué motifs, piping cord, fringing, tassles, braiding, buttons and machine or hand embroidery. Geometrically patterned fabrics and pretty prints can be used to match curtains, wall coverings or carpets. Contrast can be added to a decorative scheme by using vivid splashes of colour for cushion covers. A patchwork pattern of repeat shapes can look exciting against a background of plain-coloured furniture, and extra interest and appeal can be created with a variety of textures.

Cushion covers which can be unzipped and removed for cleaning purposes are ideal, but if you plan to wash home-made cushion covers, check that the fabric and trims are washable and colour-fast. It is a good idea to choose a crease-resistant, hard-wearing fabric where there are young children or pets.

Upholstery fabrics and loose chair covers

Upholstered furniture is expensive and should be chosen with care. Look for hard-wearing fabrics which are resistant to dirt, grease, stains and abrasion. They should be easy to clean and have a pleasant "feel". Dark-coloured, patterned or textured fabrics do not show evidence of wear and tear as easily as plain materials, and are better at disguising dirt and stains. Upholstered furniture in a living room should look warm, comfortable and inviting. Avoid cold colours such as icy blues, greens and yellows, and vibrant patterns and glaring colours which may create a restless atmosphere.

If there are young children in the family it is a good idea to look for seat cushions which can be reversed, and zipped covers which can be removed for washing. Loose caps, sleeves and back covers in matching or contrasting fabric will help to protect upholstered furniture from wear and tear and, because they are loose, they can be washed easily.

Here are some suitable upholstery fabrics.

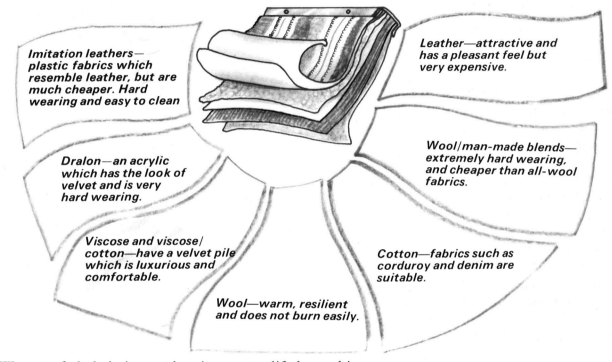

Imitation leathers— plastic fabrics which resemble leather, but are much cheaper. Hard wearing and easy to clean

Leather—attractive and has a pleasant feel but very expensive.

Dralon—an acrylic which has the look of velvet and is very hard wearing.

Wool/man-made blends— extremely hard wearing, and cheaper than all-wool fabrics.

Viscose and viscose/ cotton—have a velvet pile which is luxurious and comfortable.

Cotton—fabrics such as corduroy and denim are suitable.

Wool—warm, resilient and does not burn easily.

Worn or faded chairs can be given extra life by making or buying loose covers. If you wish to recover a chair, settee or seating unit, it is a good idea to attend an evening class on soft furnishings and seek expert help. It is important to choose a strong, pre-shrunk material which will wash well, be crease- and stain-resistant and not fray. Cotton, linen, viscose and acrylic blends are suitable. Covers can be made from plain-coloured fabrics which have an interesting textured surface. These are often decorated with piping cord, fringing or braiding. Tweeds, flowery chintz and simple all-over patterned fabrics look very effective, especially when teamed with contrasting cushions.

An alternative is to buy ready-made nylon stretch covers, which are hard wearing and easy to launder. These are available in a variety of shapes, colours and textures.

Soft furnishings on a budget

Patchworks can be made from scraps of material collected from jumble sales, charity shops, market stalls, and old but sound clothing and bedding. The remnants should be cut into even-sized pieces and then joined together by hand or machine stitching. Only select good-quality material, and check that each piece is colour-fast and shrink-resistant. Patchworks can be used for curtains, cushion covers, giant floor cushions, tablecloths, bed quilts, bedspreads, screen covers, blinds or just throwover blankets for old, worn or faded furniture.

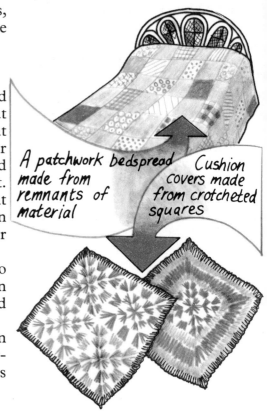

A patchwork bedspread made from remnants of material

Cushion covers made from crotcheted squares

Left-over balls of wool can be knitted or crotcheted into squares, which are then sewn together to make cushion covers, or protecting sleeves and backs for upholstered furniture and settees.

Tough fabrics such as calico, hessian and bed ticking can often be bought quite cheaply. They can be tie-dyed, decorated with appliqué motifs, braiding or fringing, and used as curtains, blinds, covers or bedspreads.

Fire hazards

Many of the furnishing fabrics in a modern home are inflammable. They will either burst into flames or burn slowly giving off toxic fumes. Wool will not burst into flames. It will char or smoulder with an acrid smell. Silk is another natural fibre which is non-inflammable. Cotton fabrics will burn, especially if they are made from a cotton/acrylic blend. Most nylons are non-inflammable and melt into a black bead-like substance. Polyester fabric is safe but polyester filling, which is used for quilts, cushions and some upholstery is inflammable.

Furniture which is made from traditional materials, such as wood, leather and horsehair, burns slowly, but many modern furniture materials are highly inflammable. Polyurethane foam-filled furniture will smoulder slowly building up heat, and then burst into flames, giving off poisonous fumes. Other plastic materials which are inflammable and used in modern furniture are PVC, polypropylene, acrylics and polyesters.

Another fire hazard in modern homes is caused by Georgian-type bow windows which have decorative panels of "bottle glass". The "bottle glass" concentrates the power of the sun's rays and can cause plastic furnishing fabrics to melt and smoulder.

Because many of the people who die in house fires are suffocated by the lethal fumes produced by burning materials, it is vital to be alert to the dangers of fabrics and furnishings catching fire. Wherever possible, choose materials which are marked "flame-resistant". Check that open fires and portable heaters are safe, and always extinguish cigarettes completely.

Think and Do

1. Give some advice on choosing curtains for the:
a. kitchen;
b. living room;
c. bathroom.
2. Explain what is meant by the following:
a. the fire hazards of modern furniture;
b. fabric finishes;
c. the "tog rating" of continental quilts.
3. List the points you would look for when choosing each of the following:
a. table linen for a growing family;
b. upholstered furniture for a living room;
c. blankets for an old age pensioner;
d. pillows for a person who has bronchitis.
4. Design a pattern for a range of co-ordinated bed linen.
5. List the advantages and disadvantages of leather imitation upholstery fabrics.
6. Collect scraps of material or wool and use them to make a cushion cover.

7. In your notebook describe how you would clean:
a. a cotton seersucker tablecloth;
b. vinyl place mats with a textured finish;
c. a pair of fibreglass curtains;
d. a candlewick bedspread.
8. Copy the following diagram into your notebook and write a suitable sentence in each of the boxes.

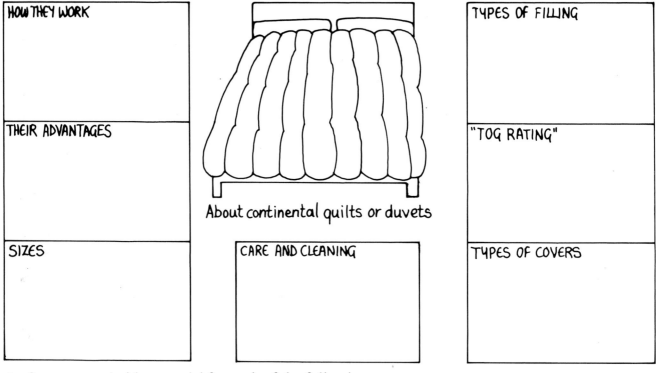

HOW THEY WORK

THEIR ADVANTAGES

SIZES

About continental quilts or duvets

CARE AND CLEANING

TYPES OF FILLING

"TOG RATING"

TYPES OF COVERS

9. Suggest a suitable material for each of the following:
a. bed sheets;
b. linings for polyester velvet curtains;
c. a tray cloth;
d. cot blankets;
e. stretch upholstery chair covers.
10. Imagine you are going to make a set of place mats. Suggest a suitable material and calculate how much you would require. In your notebook work out a design using hand or machine embroidery, appliqué motifs or bought trims. Describe the colour scheme of your place mats.